W9-ARD-568

I'm My Own M.E.
for the Pastor Without
a Minister of Education

compiled by Will Beal

LIBRARY
BRYAN COLLEGE
DAYTON, TN 37321

Convention Press
Nashville, Tennessee

WITHDRAWN
88573

Contributors

Charlotte Bowles Baker is educational director, Central Baptist Church, Alcoa, Tennessee.

Will Beal is minister of education consultant, Church Administration Department, Sunday School Board, Nashville, Tennessee.

John R. Chandler is supervisor, Church Staff Services Section, Church Administration Department, Sunday School Board, Nashville, Tennessee.

George Clark is editorial coordinator and editor of *Church Administration*, Church Administration Department, Sunday School Board, Nashville, Tennessee.

Belvin W. Cox is a preschool consultant, Sunday School Department, Sunday School Board, Nashville, Tennessee.

David W. Hayes is youth and education director, Green Hill Baptist Church, Mt. Juliet, Tennessee, and administrative manager, King, Ballow & Little, Nashville, Tennessee.

James E. Hightower, Jr. is pastoral care specialist and editor of *Proclaim*, Church Administration Department, Sunday School Board, Nashville, Tennessee.

Robert Holley is director, Church Training Department, Arkansas Baptist State Convention, Little Rock, Arkansas.

Richard E. Plyler is pastor, Patterson Grove Baptist Church, Kings Mountain, North Carolina.

© Copyright 1985 • Convention Press
All rights reserved
5290-66

Dewey Decimal Classification: 153

Subject Heading: MINISTERS // RELIGIOUS EDUCATION // CHURCH
WORK

Printed in United States of America

Church Administration Department
Sunday School Board, SBC
127 Ninth Avenue, North
Nashville, Tennessee 37234

Foreword

I'm My Own M.E. is the right book at just the right time for many reasons:

• Pastors of our twenty-one thousand smaller-in-size churches are often larger than life in spirit and vision.

• Such pastors are often looking for better ways to witness, lead, plan, educate, minister, and administer.

• Bold Mission Thrust extends worldwide the challenge of the local church.

• Volunteer leadership in the local church is the essential key to the Christian movement in our time.

• This book can become the friend and guide of a pastor in his local church leadership role.

The book is compiled and authored by Will Beal who has become a seasoned minister among the churches. He has researched, written about, and held workshops on the role of the minister of education (M.E.).

Beal has worked as a volunteer in missions and churches of all sizes and as a minister of education in larger churches with hundreds of volunteers. He now serves as a volunteer in his own church. In fact, he's my Sunday School teacher.

LLOYD ELDER
President
Sunday School Board

Preface

As a young boy I was greatly influenced by pastors of small churches. None had other staff members to assist them; so as a teenager and a college student, I helped my pastor. Later, as I was defining my call to ministry, my previous interest and love of education led me to the ministry of education.

A book to assist the pastor with the education program of the church has long been needed. A pastor must be responsible for the education program just as he is for the preaching and reaching programs. Since serving as a minister of education for twenty years and being a consultant to them for ten years, I am convinced that churches are built and sustained by a church's education program.

While compiling the book and meeting with pastors, I kept asking myself, "If I were to become the pastor of a small church, how could I best make my efforts count?" I would invest myself in the lives of a few carefully selected workers, and I would train them for his kingdom's work. Then when I moved from that church, the work would continue.

Some of the writers mention resources. Those followed by (BBS) are available at your Baptist Book Store. Those followed by (MS) may be ordered on the quarterly dated or undated order forms or from Materials Services Department, 127 Ninth Avenue, North, Nashville, Tennessee 37234.

This book has been the combined effort of many:

• the seven other writers who have written out of their real-life experiences, spending many hours on this excellent copy.

• a fellow minister, George Clark, who wrote an introduction to each chapter. You will recognize and appreciate again his Brother Goodbody style.

• Judi Hayes, the editor, who in a kind and directive way has kept us all on track. A compilation is difficult, and her skills have made it much easier.

• those pastors who shared their ministry with me.

Pastor, I hope that in the near future we can meet and discuss the ideas in this book.

Contents

Saturday evening found Brother Loner as it often did, deeply involved in the preparation of sermons to be delivered on the Lord's Day, which was fast approaching. The week had been a difficult one—including two funerals; a wedding; and a time-eroding, no-holds-barred, ongoing battle to try to keep a marriage together.

Left undone had been a hospital visit in a neighboring town, a premarital counseling session which had had to be postponed, and the reading of an article on time management which caught the parson's eye a month ago.

At times like this Brother Loner had a battle with envy as related to those brothers who had big churches and well-trained staff members to give help so sorely needed. However, there was little time for indulgence in self-pity. The flock would be waiting to be fed. Experience had taught Loner than even the best-prepared discourse from the Word would not supply the needs of some who plead for meat but perform on pablum.

Preaching was the minister's first love. Nothing brought him more satisfaction than brooding until a message was born from a passage of the Bible to which he had been led. But, alas, there was so little time for brooding these days. Most of his messages were served before he was really satisfied with their completeness.

Just now his imagination was opening up. His creative juices were beginning to flow. He could feel the Spirit's power inspiring him toward that longed-for sermon. The spell was broken by the ringing of the telephone. "Hard Rock Baptist Church. This is Brother Loner."

"Pastor, this is Mrs. Ponderous. I'm trying to finish preparation for my Sunday School lesson. I'm stumped. Surely you can help me. I know you've been to college and all, and you have time to study more than I do. Where in the Bible does it say that every tub has to sit on its own bottom?"

—George Clark

Chapter 1

What the Educational Program Can Do for Your Church

Belvin W. Cox

The Educational Program Can Establish Leadership
A universal principle is at work in groups of people, the desire of the group to have a leader. The church has traditionally expected the pastor to be that leader. You are the leader of your church.

The pastor, being the key leader in the local church, is the leader of the educational program. He is the primary educator and administrator of the educational program. He cannot lead everything himself, but he is expected to oversee the program and to enlist and develop other leaders. You, as a pastor, are at the hub of the educational process and program. If you cease to exercise that position, you cease to exercise a major portion of your call from God and the church. If you seek to enhance that position, you most nearly fulfill your call and become a developer and builder of people (see Eph. 4).

You want to do the most you can for Christ in your lifetime. You also want to build, grow, or develop the most people you can to their best potential under the Lord's leadership. You wish to grow yourself. All of the above can be done through a good Christian educational program in a local church. Your church can have a strong educational program, and you can lead it.

My ministry has been from the perspective of a pastor leading the educational program along with other primary duties. I discovered early in my ministry that a well-developed educational ministry enhances all else God called me to do. If it refines my leadership, it benefits the church.

You, the pastor, need to see the total church as an educational program. You need to see yourself as a leader and educator in the midst of this program. All that happens within the local church becomes part of the educational program as well as part of the curriculum. People, especially teachers, become the center of the program and curriculum. The key leader—you, the pastor of the local church—become the builder and strengthener of the program through the process of building other persons.

The Educational Program Can
Establish Direction for the Pastor and the Church

Discovering the dream.—Being the educator in your church will refine your agenda. The questions: Where do I wish to lead this church? What are the objectives? What resources are needed? How will we get there? are vital and need serious thought. Your visions, dreams (agenda), and the church's expectations must be brought together in an overall common direction. This then becomes the challenge of an educational program, and you are the appointed leader.

The educational program can help you seek to fulfill the realistic expectations. You can dream of seeing all persons in the community saved. You can dream of all church members' being mature Christians. You may dream of being the leading church in the association. The church may dream of being an everlasting reminder to the community of Christ's love. How can you discover and build one dream together?

One pastor of a rural church simply shared the need for a churchwide dream. The dream was used to guide the church toward its objectives and goals.

The pastor developed a questionnaire which sought to discover and/or build a dream.

Older members were asked: What was this church's dream in years past? Do you remember or did you hear why the church came into being? Do you think the church's dream is still the same as it was at its beginning?

Middle-aged members were asked: Were you aware of this church's dream when you became a member? How did you become aware of the dream? Do you think we need a dream?

Younger members were asked to write out the dream of the church as they perceived it.

All members were asked: Do we need to renew our commitment to the dream? Do we need to restate our dream? Do we need a new dream altogether? What do you think our dream should be?

The pastor then shared his desire to write a composite statement. He later read this statement to the church and asked if it reflected a dream they could pursue. After the congregation discussed, refined, and voted to accept it, the dream became the core direction for an educational program.

Each organization of the church was asked to write objectives and goals which reflected a direction toward fulfilling the dream. The pastor planned his preaching (a part of the educational program) to present the dream of the local church. The dream was consistently before the organizations and the church at work and worship.

Sunday School teachers began teaching with new direction. The Bible content became more than facts and information. Soon others were being enrolled because of the excitement of the dream. Sunday School, along with worship, became central in the educational program. Every project was considered on the reflection, Does it enhance our dream?

The WMU and Brotherhood taught missions in light of the dream and as part of the educational program. The Church Training organization began teaching and training leaders necessary to meet the needs to pursue the dream.

You can have a fresh vision which will rekindle or redirect your church. A good educational program will help the dream become a reality as it goes throughout your church and more members gain ownership.

Developing the dream.—As the educator, you will help establish objectives to clarify the dream. The dream in written form may contain objectives such as:

• To have the Bible clearly proclaimed from the pulpit and taught in the classrooms each Sunday.

• To inform regularly all church members of mission opportunities for giving and doing.

• To see that each person in the community is visited and that Christ's saving love is shared.

Many other objectives will direct your church and be reflected through the educational program.

You will certainly want to lead in setting definite goals to enhance doing your objectives. Some goals which would reflect the above objectives might be:

• To provide literature which enhances Bible study for each Sunday School teacher and member.

• To provide at least one teacher improvement clinic for all teachers this year.

• To provide opportunities for giving through special missions offerings with definite goals for home and foreign missions.

• To provide a visitation time each week with at least twenty-five persons to visit regularly.

• To use the open enrollment plan (enrolling any person who gives consent) in Sunday School and to seek to enlarge enrollment by 25 percent this year.

Resource planning will be a third process to place in motion in the agenda. Will you need books to teach program leaders? Which books? How will they help? Who should be in the class? How many leaders will be needed? Who will teach and train these leaders? Do you need an outside person to help with the training? When will the study start? Where will the study group meet? How long will the study group last? The answers to these questions will be needed for clarifying resource selection and needs.

Inform your church about what is being done to meet goals, to train leaders, and what is expected of all members to support the effort. How will they get involved?

This process will help you. It is hard work. It is a slow process many times. The real test is: Will it help you lead the church in a long-lasting work for Christ? Or will it stop with each new pastor? A good educational program is a sure way to establish a lasting result for several pastors.

The Educational Program Can
Free the Pastor for Greater Service

The educational program will multiply your ministry through others. As people are trained and understand your agenda, they will help lead the effort. A saying that has meant a lot to me is, "The one who multiplies workers is greater than the one who works." Think about this question: Would you like to be at home with your family more? You can! Share the work load of your church's ministry through a good educational program.

Once you multiply yourself, you will need to grow as a manager of people—giving direction, motivation, skills, and responsibility to others. That is delegation! Others enjoy having a part of the action when trusted and trained. Your ministry is multiplied through this effort.

You are free to be a churchman, not just a preacher. You will not only lead your congregation, but you will also enjoy being a member of the church you lead. Your own enjoyment will result in personal growth. Meanwhile, your leadership is enhanced and respected even more.

My call was clearly affirmed through this process. I realized that my call to preach was only a portion of being called to pastor a church. My call to be an educator was equal to or more than the preaching portion alone. This includes being administrator of the educational program in a local church.

In churches we often measure by Bible, bodies, baptisms, and bucks. In fact, pastors usually are programmed to look for ways to multiply these measures of success. An educational program will seek to meet people's needs. When the whole church program is person-centered, these measures of success usually take care of themselves.

Good leadership of the church educational program will allow you greater influence in all programs. It will also allow greater influence in your other tasks such as preaching and counseling. You will have a larger perspective for a Bible-centered influence in the total church's mission.

The Educational Program Can Develop Lay Leaders

One of the greatest joys for me as a pastor was to see people develop their gifts and talents. I believed my responsibility was to look for gifts in members and to help them develop those gifts for the church's good.

Pat was a quiet lady and mother of five children. Her husband was not a Christian. She had not attended church regularly for several years.

Pat was skillful at leading children. She was creative. I helped Pat to renew her fellowship with Christ and his church. Pat helped in Vacation Bible School with refreshments that summer.

Teacher enlistment time came. I talked with Pat about her gifts with children and asked her to teach. "Yes," Pat said, "if you will promise to train me for the position." I did promise to train her, and she wept. She explained: "I have wanted to teach in Sunday School since I was a teenager, but nobody has ever asked me or offered to train me. I was scared to let anybody know because I was afraid I'd be given a book and turned loose. I knew I could not teach that way."

Pat became a wonderful teacher. I learned through this experience that many people have gifts to use. Discover the prospects and develop their gifts and talents. A good educational program equips for use those gifted persons you help discover, motivate, and put in service. Pat was only one of many waiting and wanting to be used.

One valuable idea I learned from Pat was, When enlisting, provide training and expect all leaders to participate. Never just fill a slot. Do not expect a position to make a leader responsible.

Other helps for the layperson through the educational program are:

A sense of team spirit can develop in an educational program.—Christian maturity helps bring self-esteem to a person. It shows itself in reaching out to others. Self-assertiveness replaces the self-protective mode of living. Like a rock's ripple on water, it spreads and touches those farther and farther away. No advertisement for the church is better than a developing Christian leader.

Pat was a great influence for others who had known her. "Training helped her; I want it also. She can become a teacher; I will not be afraid to try."

The enlisting and training of leaders becomes a rewarding process—not a dreaded giant to tackle.—Good equipping has a way of challenging dormant gifts in people. It sets up a healthy search within persons. Much freedom to be useful is released into the church's life. That in itself enhances the educational program. Remember that the whole life of a church is educational and each experience and every person are part of the process.

The pastor becomes a trusted friend, a facilitator for personal growth, and a strong leader.—He sees in an intimate way the struggles of his people. Through the educational process the pastor is educated about his people. He becomes a better shepherd, preacher, counselor, and friend to laypersons.

The pastor becomes a role model to those he guides in the educational process.—As a layperson receives care, guidance, training, and other equipping, he is also learning how to become an equipper to others. The process has a multiplying effect which enhances people building and church family ties. Laypersons should be encouraged to pass their training on to others.

An educational program gives the layperson an avenue of relationship to the pastor.—He then can have open avenues for good rapport with key leaders. The educator can respond more quickly to the needs in the church family. The needs of members are met promptly.

Ken was the Sunday School director in a small church. He had little background for his position, but he served the best he could. The pastor spent some time with Ken each week talking and praying about the purpose, plans, and problems of the Sunday School. Together they planned for improvements such as training and how to use the records for outreach.

Out of their visits came a plan to have a visitation program. Each week one class member would represent each youth and adult class for visitation. Other class members were also encouraged to help. An outreach leader assigned members different persons to visit weekly. Each week in Sunday School members who visited during the week shared their experiences.

Enrollment soon began to increase as this simple plan began to reach prospects. Class members began to be enthusiastic about visiting and did not wait until "their turn" to go visiting. Visitation night was a good experience. The pastor was having more and more open doors into other church organizations to help leaders strengthen the work. Many doors in the community were opened to him also.

Better educational budgeting will result in touching more lives through the educational program.—Questions that should be considered include: How much of the budget goes for training leaders? Is leadership training done on a regular basis? Do we advertise training events? Should we use inside teachers or outside training leaders?

As a pastor, I led the church to make available budgeted funds for training all church leaders. The ongoing training of key leaders will have a greater impact on the educational program than money spent elsewhere. It offers returns in the church better than any other expense. Deacons, Sunday School or Church Training directors and teachers, WMU and Brotherhood leaders all need training at times. The church should see that all willing leaders get training and pay for such training when appropriate.

In a former church I asked each leader to think of the goals that should be met in the coming year. The directors of each section of an organization took all the suggestions and compiled them. The adult teachers got together with the adult director. WMU leaders got together with the WMU director. In a small church, the whole Sunday School leadership could meet together and think about needs the Sunday School could meet.

Each organization estimates the cost of its proposals. They list the needs along with costs in the order they feel they should be accomplished. These requests should be given to the budget committee to compile and bring before the church for voting to fund them. The budget committee may ask a director to meet with them and explain the importance of a proposal and how it supports the church's goals and objectives.

The Educational Program Can
Lead to a Balanced Emphasis

Many churches with a pastor as the only staff have had good preaching while stagnating with malnutrition. A good educational program will bring balance, because preaching is seen as one spoke of a good educational wheel, not the whole wheel (see Eph. 4:11-12). In _The Minister of Education as Educator,_ (BBS) we read: "Education is essential to Christianity. . . . A church is not the church, as Jesus established and commissioned it, if it does not educate. Education is one of the basic functions of a church."[1]

I became a better preacher while strengthening my responsibility to be a teacher and an educator. One example is my study of child development while trying to work better with my preschool teachers. It made a real impact on my biblical understanding and even the needs of adults in my church.

I appealed more clearly to the lost and could feed the saints. Evangelism and Christian maturity are mutual encouragers, not enemies. Quality Christian education and reaching into the world go together.

I promoted the organizations much better after working with their needs. I developed empathy which helped me become interested in their efforts. I realized that all were part of the church and accomplished a part of the church's total educational program. When one is strengthened, all get stronger. The spiritual temperature of the church will not go any higher than the spiritual temperature of the pastor. A chain is held together by the strong links. Guide your leaders to be strong links.

The Educational Program Supports the Church's Ministry

By its very nature the church is a ministry. We are priests. We are ministers. We are disciples of the greatest minister who ever lived. We see in Christ the essence of a ministering God, full of grace, mercy, and trust.

Picture his path across the pages of our New Testament, and think on the full measure of his ministry. This is the ministry he left with his disciples, from those early chosen apostles to those seated by you in church on Sunday.

Gaines Dobbins said, "A church that does not minister to human need has abandoned the New Testament pattern."[2] Jesus established his church as a servant to this world of need. To deny our servant status is to deny the servant of God who modeled the servant's role as God wanted it lived out in his church. He has sent us to this world as the Father sent him.

The pastor of a church bears a responsibility to model the maturing Christian life. This is the essence of the Great Commission. It is all tied together around the effectiveness of the educational program of a church, for all a church does is educative. Better Christian servants build better churches that grow more maturing servants.

Caring for persons in their needs is a never-ending task. The church's mission ever widens. Life goes on with endless situations through which the church seeks insights for living out its mission. Gaines Dobbins said, "Life presents the problems, and a church is the school where the answers are to be found."[3]

The local church is one of many caring congregations seeking to reach the whole world with the good news. The educa-

tional programs of local churches determine to a great extent
how far into the world the good news will penetrate.

The Educational Program Can Enhance Church Fellowship
Fellowship is more than eating together. That simply provides
an opportunity for many close friends to have fellowships.
You could eat with people and have no fellowship.

Fellowship development should be conscientiously woven
into every area of the educational program. When we have
committee meetings, worship, classes, special training, or any
other event, fellowship should be strengthened. Births,
deaths, anniversaries, marriages, graduations, and other special events should call for bonds of true fellowship to be evi-
denced in your church.

In my last pastorate the church had a real gift for turning
lots of meetings into fellowships. The members enjoyed one
another. The hospitality committee was probably the most
active and busiest committee in the whole church. This committee saw its responsibilities as a ministry in the church and
through the church to the community. The members really
served as a joint between two body members many times. The
beauty of this was that they knew they served that purpose
and planned to do it well as servants to the church. They were
serious and excited about it.

They had a reception (sometimes with only lemonade and
cookies) almost anytime a group presentation happened. It
wasn't for "visiting" groups only but rather a celebration with
any group effort. Groups were made to feel important to the
whole church. All ages were invited and participated in saying thank you.

Organizational programs were representations of the
church's mission. Many times programs were jointly spon-
sored across organizational divisions. Likewise ministries
were planned so that different groups shared the responsibilities. The Lottie Moon Christmas offering was the
church's responsibility, led by the WMU and Brotherhood.

Programming was not always age graded. Older members

made it a point to enlist youth to aid them. Youth likewise asked the elderly to be a part of their togetherness, even to serve in some way. Fellowship knew no age barriers in this congregation.

Jesus can be identified with such times in his earthly ministry. These are the times we can touch lives for good and for changes to take place—that's educational!

The Educational Program Can
Challenge Less Active Church Members

Within each church there is usually a large group of uninvolved members. Many times these persons need a challenge to discipleship. Many have never been invited or instructed to own a piece of the action. An educational program should seek to draw out and involve this group and to use their gifts.

First, the program should give evidence to these persons that Christ has title to his church. Regularly involved members should be excited about the evidences of God at work in their church.

Second, the educational program gives inactive, marginal members the feeling of "our" church—a sense of partnership in the church life. Even if they do not share much responsibility for it, they are still proud of their church. This attitude shows up many times, especially in smaller churches, when a crisis affects the church. Many inactive members then take part.

Third, the educational program opens lines of communication. Churches may have a newsletter, grapevine, or other means of communication. The better the educational program, the better the communication lines throughout the church family and into the community.

This is good. We communicate best and most with those with whom we have some relationship in the church. A better communication network means more openness to one another. It means more avenues to get the good news out to the grass-roots members and to the church community. It means finding prospects for Bible study. It has an unmistakable drawing power when used for good in the educational program. It cultivates those in the community we are trying to reach.

The Educational Program Can Lead to Church Growth

An educational program develops believers. The church is a school of life. Both quality and quantity are definite results of Christian education.

Quality and quantity are allies, not enemies. In fact, real quality affects the quantity and attracts like quality. Then quantity must redirect the quality. They stand together when at their best in Christian education.

I did most of my pastoring in small churches as the only staff person. Of course, my wife was staff without really being classified as such. In those churches, I figured out they meant staff when saying, "She's the pastor's wife."

My wife, Barbara, and I worked together closely to train and undergird the educational program in those churches. We divided the leadership training responsibilities. Barbara taught preschool and children's teachers, and I taught youth and adult teachers. We scheduled the training during the Church Training hour every Sunday night for one quarter. Sunday School, Church Training, music, and missions leaders for these age groups were invited along with potential workers and parents of the age groups. After the three months of training, we worked side by side with the leaders during their sessions for the next three months.

It was great to see growth take place as leaders began to understand their age group, their organization, their materials from the Baptist Sunday School Board, and their mission as teachers. It was rewarding to watch teachers mature through associational, state, and other training opportunities.

The greatest adventure was to see them study books on their own through the Church Study Course system and even in local colleges or special community education classes. Some found God's call for their life's vocation.

The ultimate blessing was to see budgeted each year an extraordinary teacher's conference for the whole church. Many times other nearby churches were invited because our people wanted to share good training. Many smaller training events were held throughout the year.

The church was really growing qualitatively. That was tremendous! How about the numbers? Space doesn't permit all details, but let's look at one area—preschool.

Barbara worked at teaching and modeling each part of a preschool department. She made temporary equipment to furnish the department and engaged the teachers to help—hands-on teaching! She taught several books: One on child development, *Understanding Today's Preschoolers*, (BBS); one on organization, *Basic Preschool Work*, (BBS); and one on guidance in teaching preschoolers, *How to Guide Preschoolers* (BBS).

Barbara then went into the two departments for one month each and demonstrated the role of each teacher. She then turned the duties back to the teachers fully and became ready to help if they needed her.

You know what happened? Sure you do! Those teachers moved their preschoolers from the damp basement to a more suitable area with proper room and light. They made and purchased permanent equipment for their departments after which they hosted an open house for the whole church.

You guessed it. Both departments were soon full. Two more were started, equipped, staffed, and trained; and ages were divided again. One enthusiastic teacher of three-year-olds said, "I'll be glad when we promote again, I have already located enough children to fill this room again."

That's not all! The young adults class grew also. They had twelve on roll with an attendance of about six. Parents got tired of running back home and coming to get children later. They started staying for Sunday School. The young adult department reached twenty-seven on roll with eighteen average attendance for their class.

Church Training was now growing numerically because

people had become accustomed to coming on Sunday night. We offered the regular Church Training curriculum, while special training was going on for leaders.

Good education does help the church grow both in quality and in numbers. I challenge you to learn through conference opportunities and go back to your church to share your training with your leaders. Then encourage them to go, and go with them, to good conferences. Put into practice what is learned. Have a meeting the night after a conference, and allow your people to share what they have learned. Decide together how you can implement this training into your church program. It will change your church!

You, as pastor, are the educator in charge of the educational program in your church. With a good educational program, dreams become reality and the Bible becomes the living Word in the midst of a church on mission. The church awaits your leadership; you can do it! Start today! May God bless you and many others through you.

---

[1] Allen W. Graves, "Education as a Function of a Church," in *The Minister of Education as Educator*, Will Beal, comp. (Nashville: Convention Press, 1979), p. 4.

[2] Gaines S. Dobbins, *A Ministering Church* (Nashville: Broadman Press, 1960), p. 12.

[3] Ibid., p. 14.

Brother Loner slipped into the auditorium for the opening exercise. He tried to do so as often as possible to indicate his support of the Sunday School program in general and of Frank Fumbler in particular. Frank was the Sunday School director. He was making real progress in his assigned task. For example, he had got to the point of referring to himself as director as opposed to superintendent. The struggle had not been easy.

He had also waged a worthy battle in getting the attenders to be on time for the Sunday event. More then half of them were arriving at least seconds before the appointed time. Most of the others were going directly to their classrooms. The exception was the Tardy family whose five members always arrived late and went all the way down to the second seat from the front.

Frank was good with announcements and had been known to do a fair job of leading the group in singing the opening hymn on those rare occasions when Thelma Thrush was late or did not arrive at all. But honesty demanded the pastor privately to admit that bringing a devotional was not Frank's best skill.

Brother Loner had experienced some small victory in making Frank aware of the Sunday School resources especially designed to meet his needs to lead the opening period. Frank had agreed to try the material. The pastor had come especially to see how much the use of such materials would help the general mood of the morning.

The last notes of the hymn were dying just as Brother Loner sat down. Frank rose to begin his presentation. "Thank you for that good singing. We're glad all of you could come today. We'll have our prayer requests right after I share a devotional thought with you." Loner basked in the warm glow of satisfaction.

"The preacher gave me a book to help me with these things; but as much as I hate to admit it, I couldn't find it this morning. So I'm going to read this piece I thought was real good. I found it in a book of devotionals I got from Brother Beller. I'm sure most of you hear him on TV on Sunday mornings."

—George Clark

Chapter 2

Using Available Resources to Get the Work Done

Robert Holley

An old preacher was struggling with his preparation for a sermon on stewardship. He left his study and drove down a country road. As he drove along, he observed one particular farm that stood out above all the others. It was well kept with beautiful fences and abundant crops. It apparently was a great source of pride to its owner. He noticed the farmer standing near the fence beside the road and stopped to compliment him on his beautiful farm. The preacher said, "The Lord has certainly given you a beautiful place here." The farmer, thanking the preacher for the compliment, said, "It certainly is a good farm and a pretty place, but you should have seen this place when he had it all to himself."

The old preacher had his sermon for Sunday. He realized that God had given to every other farmer along that road the same kind of soil and the same sunshine and rain. The difference was the way in which this farmer managed the resources available to him.

A pastor's role has been described as (1) proclaiming the gospel, (2) ministering to people, and (3) leading the church to accomplish its objectives. As you seek to give leadership to your church, especially to its educational program, one of your most important skills will be your ability to manage the resources available to you.

As a pastor, you have many responsibilities and many claims on your time and energies. You must choose how you use the time and energy God has given you so as to accomplish the greatest good in your ministry and lead your church in its ministry. You want to help your church members develop an effective educational program that will reach people, teach them God's Word, win them to faith in Christ, and guide them to grow toward maturity in Christ—equipping them to do all the things Jesus commanded us to do. As a pastor with many other responsibilities, you can do this only as you become a good manager of resources.

There are basically five kinds of resources available to you: (1) people, (2) time, (3) facilities and equipment, (4) money, and (5) materials. Each of these will be discussed, and in some cases you will be referred to other materials that deal with these resources in greater detail.

Working with and Through People

Aside from the leadership of the Holy Spirit, no other resource is as important as people in maintaining an effective educational program. The way you work with and through people and groups in your church can greatly affect the total program of your church. You can greatly multiply yourself and your ministry as you work with those people who serve in various leadership roles. Moses learned early in his leadership role the need to multiply himself by working with and through others who could serve and minister with him (see Ex. 18). He discovered it was not only the best way to conserve his time and energies but also the only way to get the job done.

Your role as an equipper has already been discussed in chapter 1. Work closely with your church leaders as they plan for an effective church educational program. The following suggestions are offered to help you as you work with key leaders in your church.

Assist the church nominating committee in selecting and enlisting leaders.—The church nominating committee has the responsibility of discovering, selecting, enlisting, and recommending to the church those persons who will fill all the volunteer leadership positions. This includes those who are leaders in Sunday School, Church Training, Woman's Missionary Union, Brotherhood, and the Music Ministry. In addition, the nominating committee has responsibility for enlisting church media library workers; those who serve in church recreation leadership; those who will serve on other church committees; and the general church officers such as clerk, trustees, treasurer, and moderator.

It is obvious that this committee has an important task. The way this committee functions and the choices it makes greatly influence your church's educational program.

By working closely with the nominating committee, you can exert leadership and influence that will indirectly strengthen the total church program. It is important that the committee lead in the enlistment of committed, capable people who have the potential to become good leaders. It is also important that the process of enlistment be appropriate and effective if leaders are to take seriously their responsibilities.

You can do three things to help assure the enlistment of good leadership in your church: (1) Guide your church to select appropriate persons to serve on the nominating committee. (2) Train the nominating committee to do its job well. (3) Work with the nominating comittee on a regular basis. Secure copies of *The Church Nominating Committee* (MS) for each committee member. Use this booklet to train the committee and guide members in their work.

Work closely with the Church Council to plan, coordinate, and evaluate your church program.—Every church has a church staff. That's right! Even in a one-staff church, a church with only a pastor, the pastor can have a church staff. In such a church the staff is the Church Council. These are the key leaders who share the greatest responsibility for leading the church in its various ministries. In most churches these include the Sunday School, Church Training, Brotherhood, WMU, and Music Ministry directors. These five persons, along with the chairman of deacons and the pastor, serve on the Church Council. If there are other staff members, full-time or part-time, they should also serve on the Church Council. Directors of church service programs, such as the director of the church media library and the director of recreation services, also serve on the council. Certain committee chairpersons also serve on the Church Council; these include such committees as stewardship, evangelism, and missions. Other committee chairpersons attend meetings only when matters related to their work are discussed.

Working closely with this group of key leaders can greatly strengthen and multiply your ministry. This group, meeting together on a regular basis (preferably once a month), can help you evaluate your church program, plan projects and actions to help strengthen every area of your work, and help coordinate your program so you achieve the maximum results with the resources available to you. It is this group that will lead your church to establish church objectives, determine priorities, and plan an annual church calendar.

Each member of the Church Council wears two hats. Each is responsible for the program he or she leads. Each is also concerned for and committed to the total church program. These key leaders, working together regularly, can be mutually supportive, and together they can strengthen all your church is attempting to accomplish.

A functioning Church Council provides you an excellent opportunity to exert influence and leadership that can affect every aspect of your church education program. Secure copies of *The Church Council Handbook* (BBS) for each member of the committee, and use this resource to train the members to function as a group.

Give encouragement and guidance to other key leaders in the church.—As pastor, you are in a unique position to offer encouragement and guidance to other groups of key leaders in your church and thus strengthen your educational program. Included are the key leaders in Sunday School, Church Training, WMU, Brotherhood, and Music Ministry.

You do not need to be thoroughly familiar with all the work of each of these programs and all of their materials and methods. However, they must know of your interest in their work and that they have your encouragement and support. When these key groups meet for planning, you can encourage them by being present and offering counsel and encouragement to them in their work. Volunteer leaders in a church need to know they are valued and their service is appreciated. No one can communicate this better than the pastor. It is important for them to know they have your support.

Work with other groups on behalf of the educational program. These include the stewardship committee, the property and space committee, and the church media library. Those persons who serve in these areas can help provide funds, facilities, equipment, and other resources needed in the educational program. You, as pastor, can make these persons aware of educational needs.

Be alert to opportunities to give assistance and encouragement to key leaders in your church. Spend an hour with your Sunday School director, sharing your concerns about outreach and Bible Study and offering guidance and encouragement. Don't miss opportunities to multiply yourself through important key leaders in your church.

Discover people resources beyond your own church.—Most churches find that they must occasionally draw on resources outside the church. This is especially true in the training of leaders for your educational program. Find resource persons who have the training and experience to help your church do what it could not otherwise do with its own resources.

Other churches in your area may have well-trained leaders who would be happy to help train some of your leaders in certain program areas. The finest that is available in any church should be available to every church.

Your associational office is another good source of assistance. Associational leaders are trained to help the churches and frequently are just waiting to be asked. Encourage the leaders in your educational program to take advantage of training opportunities offered by your association, or invite associational leaders to come to your church for training sessions planned specifically for your church. Consult your associational calendar for those events that are designed to meet the needs of your church, and take advantage of these opportunities.

Your state convention frequently offers training events that can greatly strengthen your educational program. Some are especially helpful to the pastor, while others are for volunteer leaders who staff various church programs. Consult your state convention calendar for those events to be conducted in your area, and exert your leadership to encourage participation.

You may also request the assistance of your state convention staff in your church. Most state conventions have consultants who are available to give personal assistance to churches in specific areas of the educational program.

Other denominational resources are available for leadership training beyond your church. Some of the best training opportunities available are found at Ridgecrest and Glorieta Conference Centers. Well-trained and experienced resource persons offer training for leaders in every area of the church education program. In addition to developing skills, leaders find the challenge and inspiration essential for the job their church has assigned them. For information about the Conference Centers write: Conference Center Division, Baptist Sunday School Board, 127 Ninth Avenue, North, Nashville, Tennessee 37234, or phone (615) 251-2293.

People resources, those in your church and those beyond your church, can be your greatest asset as you lead in your church educational program. To neglect these key persons would be poor stewardship of one of our finest resources.

Making the Most of Your Time
Time is another valuable resource, one that must be managed well if the objectives of the church are to be accomplished. Time, like money, must be budgeted if it is to accomplish the greatest good. Time is also like money in that it can easily slip away from us without our knowing where it went. A pastor cannot do everything he needs or wants to do. Neither can a

church do everything it might wish to do during a given year. Responsible decisions must be made by the pastor and the church regarding how the time available will be invested. If you and your church can recognize time as one of your most valuable resources and plan carefully for its use, then the hours, days, weeks, and months God gives you will be fruitful; and together you will begin to see your dreams realized.

The pastor's time must be budgeted.—If giving leadership to your church's educational program is one of your priority concerns, it will require an investment of your time. Like most pastors, you may feel that there are not enough hours to get done those things that must be done. However, it could be that you are spending your time in a way that does not get maximum return on your investment. Here are some suggestions that may be helpful to you in managing your time:

• Base your priorities on the needs and concerns of your church. Allocate your time according to these priorities.

• Set goals that reflect what you want to accomplish this week, this month, this year.

• Make a list daily of tasks you plan to accomplish and arrange them in order of priority. Check off the tasks as you complete them and carry over to the next day any tasks not completed. This practice provides a great sense of accomplishment as tasks are completed, and it gives a sense of direction to the way you spend your day.

• Delegate responsibilities to other persons or groups, instruct them in their task, provide them the resources they need, and leave the responsibility with them.

• Recognize that time will not allow you faithfully to discharge your responsibility if you spend time on tasks for which someone else is responsible or on tasks that should be delegated to someone else. A pastor cannot do the work of the treasurer or the property and space committee, the secretary or the custodian and still have time to be the pastor. Spend the greatest amount of your time doing those things which only you as pastor can do. Delegate other tasks to appropriate persons who can be equipped for them.

A pastor who sincerely desires to give leadership to the church education program must manage his time well in order to do so. As pastor, you should see time spent helping to strengthen the educational program as one of the most productive ways you could spend your time and one of the best ways to multiply yourself and your ministry.

For additional help with time management, see *Getting on Top of Your Work* (BBS) by Brooks Faulkner, chapter 7, and *Basic Small Church Administration* (BBS), chapter 6.

The church's time must be budgeted.—Just as a pastor must budget his time, a church should budget its time. A church budget serves as a guide for using available funds in the most productive way. A church calendar serves the same purpose as the church plans how it will use the time available during the year.

A pastor can lead a church to address some of its critical educational needs by providing input into the calendar planning process. The Church Council, discussed earlier, is responsible for annual calendar planning.

The priority needs and concerns of your church should be reflected in the projects, events, and special emphases that are scheduled on your church calendar. The calendar is a statement of how your church plans to use its time during a given year.

As pastor, you have an opportunity to work with Church Council members to include projects and emphases that can strengthen your educational program. You will want to schedule those events that will strengthen your efforts in outreach, Bible study, training, missionary education, stewardship, evangelism, and leadership development.

Some of the events or projects you will want to consider include January Bible Study, Baptist Doctrine Study, Christian Home Week, Vacation Bible School, and Sunday School Preparation Week. These are annual events in many churches.

You can also benefit your educational program greatly by including in your calendar those events outside your church that are offered for your leaders. Unless you can anticipate these projects and include them in your calendar, you will find difficulty guarding the time so your leaders can take advantage of these valuable sources of help. Secure a copy of your associational and state convention calendars before you begin your calendar planning.

As you plan your church calendar, remember that you are planning how your church will spend one of its most valuable resources. Plan carefully with the priority needs of your church and community in mind.

Using Facilities and Equipment

A church's educational program often takes on the shape of its buildings. You can influence the effectiveness of your educational program significantly by leading your church to provide and maintain adequately the facilities and equipment appropriate to each age group in the church.

Some churches need additional space to accommodate present or anticipated growth. Others need to improve their use of the space available in order to meet the requirements of each age group. For some churches better maintenance is the most pressing need. The amount of space available, its arrangement, and the maintenance of facilities have a significant influence on the effectiveness and quality of a church's educational program. The following suggestions may help you as you seek to lead your church to provide adequate facilities and equipment for your educational program.

Work with the key leaders of your church (Church Council) to assess your present and future space needs.—Walk through your building with the leaders who work in the various age groups. Determine whether your present space is adequate in light of your enrollment and attendance records and in light of your growth potential. Try to determine if additional space is needed or if there is a better way to allocate existing space.

Consult *Christian Education Handbook* (BBS), chapter 6, for guidelines in determining space needs. See also *Managing the Business Affairs of the Church* (BBS) and *Church Property and Building Guidebook* (BBS). Also consult your state church architecture consultant about available space.

Share your findings and recommendations with appropriate groups such as the church property and space committee, stewardship (or budget) committee, building committee, or long-range planning committee. You can help tremendously with planning for present and future needs if you lead your church to make a careful assessment of its facilities.

Inventory the furnishings and equipment in your educational space to determine if they are adequate for each age group.— Check on such items as chairs, tables, chalkboards, tackboards, storage cabinets, record players, projectors, and maps. Note items that should be repaired or replaced. List items that are needed so you can begin to formulate recommendations for consideration in budget planning.

A good educational program needs furnishings, equipment and teaching aids, and department and class arrangement appropriate for each age group. For suggested room arrangements and a list of suggested furnishings and equipment for each age group, see *Christian Education Handbook,* pp. 156-60.

Lead your church to make adequate provision in the budget for proper maintenance of facilities and equipment.—This should include provisions for both housekeeping and repairs. It is poor stewardship of resources for a church to invest large sums of money in facilities and equipment and fail to maintain them properly.

Spending Dollars Wisely

A dollar spent one place can't be spent some place else. This expression underscores the need for churches to manage their financial resources wisely. As pastor, you can help your church manage its allocation of funds to meet the needs of your educational program. One of your best opportunities to influence the allocation of funds for your educational program is by working closely with your stewardship (or budget) committee as they do annual budget planning. You can influence the budget planning process in several ways.

Guide your church to select stewardship committee members who are familiar with the total program of the church.—They will be more sensitive to the needs relative to the educational program and other programs of the church.

Formulate, with the help of some of your key leaders, recommendations to be presented to the stewardship committee.—Included should be funds for such items as literature, supplies, equipment, furnishings, and leadership training.

Adequate literature, including teaching helps, is essential to a good educational program. Provide adequate materials for your leaders, including resource kits, lesson commentaries, and other teaching aids.

Funds allocated for leadership training will enable leaders to attend conference centers, workshops, or other training opportunities that will greatly improve their leadership skills. Money invested in developing leaders may be one of the best investments your church could make in its future. Review your church budget to determine how your funds are allocated. If you discover you are spending more on floor wax than on leadership training, you may want to help your church examine its priorities. It would not be unreasonable for many churches to allocate 2-3 percent of their budget to leadership training. How can you better use your influence to multiply your ministry through other persons?

By working with the stewardship committee to secure adequate funds for your educational program, you can help improve the effectiveness of your leaders at every age level and influence every facet of your church's witness and ministry.

Selecting and Using Appropriate
Curriculum Materials and Related Resources

The careful selection and proper use of materials, both leader and member materials, are essential. These materials largely determine the methodology and the content of your educational program. The proper use of appropriate materials by skilled leaders has the potential to change lives, mold attitudes, develop concepts, impart knowledge, and influence behavior. As you lead your church to select appropriate curriculum materials and help your leaders learn to use them effectively, you will strengthen your educational program and the lives of those persons involved.

No pastor can be expected to become thoroughly familiar with the format, content, and methodology of every available curriculum piece for all church programs. In fact, some pastors are bewildered by the wide variety of materials available. However, you can become aware of the materials available for use in the various programs of your church, the age group for which they are designed, and how to secure them.

Some basic resources will help you as you work with key leaders in your church in selecting appropriate materials. Included in this listing are materials related to Sunday School, Church Training, Woman's Missionary Union, Brotherhood, Music Ministry, church media library, church recreation, and the Church Council.

*General materials related to
the total church educational program*

A Church on Mission (BBS), compiled by Reginald McDonough, contains a comprehensive study of the nature and functions of a church and the work of each of its programs and organizations, including an overview of each area of the church educational program.

Church Materials Catalog, published annually by the Sunday School Board and distributed without cost to pastors, church staff members, and denominational leaders, contains a listing and description of all dated and undated curriculum materials published by the Sunday School Board, including curriculum outlines for the current year. It includes materials for Sunday School, Church Training, church music, church media library, church recreation, church architecture, pastoral and deacon ministries, family ministry, stewardship, student ministries, weekday education, and church secretaries. It also contains a description of materials for current emphases such as January Bible Study, Baptist Doctrine Study, Foreign and Home Mission studies, and Christian

Home Week, and a complete listing of Church Study Course books and diploma plans.

Church Study Course Catalog contains a complete listing and description of all books in the Church Study Course and requirements for the various diplomas available through the Church Study Course system. The Church Study Course offers a wide variety of materials for training leaders in every area of your church program in addition to general materials for Christian development. Materials in the Church Study Course catalog cover twenty-three subject areas. This can be a valuable resource to use as you guide your leaders to complete the training courses they need.

Christian Education Handbook, compiled by Bruce P. Powers, is a comprehensive resource book presenting the work of all church programs, including helps related to organization, leadership, facilities, equipment, planning, enlistment, and leadership training.

Basic administrative books related to church programs and services

For each of the five program organizations (Sunday School, Church Training, WMU, Brotherhood, and Music Ministry), there is a basic administration guide—a book setting forth the basic tasks, organization, leadership, and curriculum needs of the program. These can serve as reference materials for you when you need specific information. You will want to encourage your leaders to complete the study of those related to their assignment. Also included in the list are the basic administration books for church media library and church recreation.

• Sunday School: *Basic Sunday School Work* (BBS)
• Church Training: *Equipping Disciples Through Church Training* (BBS)
• Woman's Missionary Union: *Woman's Missionary Union Manual* (BBS)
• Brotherhood: *The Purpose and Plan of Baptist Brotherhood* (BBS)
• Music Ministry: *Building an Effective Music Ministry*

(BBS)
• Church Media Library: *A Church Media Library at Work* (BBS)
• Church Recreation: *A Guide to Church Recreation* (BBS)
All these materials are included in the Church Study Course and will fulfill part of the requirements for diplomas for leaders who serve in these areas of your church program.

Program periodicals

General administrative helps are available in quarterly periodicals for pastors and program leaders. These materials should also be available to the director and key leaders of your educational program. These periodicals contain some valuable articles that speak specifically to the pastor. These periodicals offer the best way to keep up-to-date on the work of each area of the educational program.
• Sunday School: *Sunday School Leadership* (MS)
• Church Training: *Church Training* (MS)
• Woman's Missionary Union: *Royal Service*
• Brotherhood: *Brotherhood Builder*
• Music Ministry: *The Church Musician* (MS)
• Church Media Library: *Media: Library Services Journal* (MS)
• Church Recreation: *Church Recreation Magazine* (MS)

Planning helps

The key leaders of each area of your church program need materials to guide them in planning their work on an annual basis. The following materials will be helpful as you lead them to plan their work more effectively:
• Sunday School: *Sunday School Plan Book* (BBS)
• Church Training: *Church Training* (June issue) (MS)
• Woman's Missionary Union: *The WMU Year Book* (BBS)
• Brotherhood: *Brotherhood Builder* (July issue)
• Music Ministry: *Music Ministry Plan Book* (BBS)
• Church Council: *Church Administration* (May issue) (MS)
The listing of resource materials does not begin to include all the materials available for a church educational program. These should be seen as reference materials to which you can turn when you have a specific question or need. These basic

materials list and describe many other curriculm materials that can enrich your total educational program. If you have access to the items listed here and will acquaint yourself with these materials, you can give valuable assistance to leaders in your church and influence greatly your educational program.

When God called Moses to a place of leadership, Moses felt inadequate for the task. The Lord asked Moses, "What is that in thine hand?" (Ex. 4:2). Moses replied that it was a rod. Under God's leadership, that rod was used to strengthen Moses's leadership position and to enable him to do the task to which God had called him. Properly managing available resources can greatly enrich the church's educational program, strengthen the pastor's leadership, and multiply his ministry. It's the best way to get the job done.

"Good morning, Pastor," the voice on the telephone whined. "This is Olive Overload. I couldn't help hearing what you said in your message yesterday about how badly our church needs workers in some of the children's classes. I haven't been able to sleep all night. The Lord must be dealing with me about taking one of those groups. I just had to call and tell you of my decision."

At times like this Brother Loner fought an impulse to cut his wrists with his plastic letter opener. Olive was at it again. One of the most frequently heard from members of Hard Rock Baptist Church, Olive was the mother of five children and the proprietress of at least the second dirtiest house in the church. She was also the church's chronic volunteer.

Brother Loner had sometimes speculated at just what combination of guilt feelings made it utterly impossible for Olive to get past an invitation of any kind. Loner knew that any appeal for people to become involved in outreach would press Olive into telephone calling and doorbell ringing. And honestly, she was the last person in the flock he would have chosen to meet prospects. Her unkempt appearance, whiny voice, and martyr complex would likely have turned Saul of Tarsus back at the Damascus city limits sign.

One of the great unsolved mysteries of church vocations work for Loner was how the persons he really wanted to respond conveniently sidestepped his most fervent appeal, while Olive threw herself at the foot of the altar at even the slightest hint of a need anywhere in the church.

—George Clark

Chapter 3

Working with the Volunteer

Will Beal

From the days of the early church, the volunteer has carried the load. Even those who led in the building of the early church were volunteers or at the most bivocational. Paul and the disciples received little if any income for their labor. Was not Christ himself a volunteer? Think of the church today, if you can, without volunteers. Today millions in our churches freely offer their services.

Look at the many organizations in our country today that depend on volunteers. What would our hospitals, civic organizations, charitable institutions, and political system be without volunteers?

The pastor also needs the volunteer. Many pastors may think the burden of the success of a church's ministry is totally his responsibility. Through the volunteer the pastor can share the ministry. The pastor succeeds as he encourages and enables others to get involved. As they become involved, he is freer to do those tasks that are particularly assigned to him as pastor. The successful pastor is a willing delegator. The pastor should look at everything he does and ask, "Who else could be doing this?"

The volunteer will rebel if he is not a part of the church's ministry. Staff ministers rob the church member of an essential ingredient needed in Christian growth if they are unwilling to share the work.

Here is an exercise that will help you evaluate your willingness to delegate.

Rate Your Ability to Share Responsibility

Check the answer that best describes how you are now functioning. Compare your responses to the answer sheet and add up your score. Then study the answers on the answer sheet.

1. How often do you talk with volunteer church leaders whom you supervise?

   Daily ____ Weekly ____ Monthly ____

2. Do you discuss the problems they are having in doing their jobs?

   Always ____ Often ____ Seldom ____

3. Do you explain the things the workers should do in carrying out church projects?

   Always ____ Often ____ Seldom ____

4. Do you expect the volunteers you supervise to carry out your instructions exactly?

   Yes ____ No ____

5. Does it bother you that many people never are able to do things the right way?

   Yes ____ No ____

6. Are the people you supervise in church organizations capable of making the decisions that need to be made?

   Yes ____ No ____ Doubtful ____

7. Do you help your people out with a tough assignment

   Always ____ Often ____ Seldom ____

when they encoun-
ter a problem?

8. Do you always like   Yes ___ No ___
   to see things done
   fast and right?

9. Do your workers   Always ___ Often ___ Seldom ___
   feel free to ask why
   something must be
   done a certain way?

10. How do your volun-   Enthusiastically ___ Indifferently ___
    teer workers react
    to the programs
    your church con-
    ducts?·

                       YOUR SCORE ___

Answers

1. *Weekly* —If you are talking with your volunteer leaders daily, chances are you are oversupervising them to the point that they have no freedom to work responsibly. Monthly is too seldom in any full-time church situation.

2. *Always*—The person who shares responsibility sees his job in building people, not just getting a job done. The volunteer's development and the overcoming of problems are more important than job performance. The focus is on the worker and not primarily on the job.

3. *Seldom*—The person who must explain detailed instructions has not involved the workers in the planning and, therefore, has not shared responsibility, which is more than just sharing the work.

4. *No*—Too detailed instructions leave no room for shared responsibility. Don't demand observance of the letter but the spirit of your guidance.

5. *No*—If you marked yes, chances are you aren't willing to let your workers pursue their course of action if it doesn't coin-

cide with yours. In shared responsibility, there can be several right ways.

6. *Yes*—Shows that you have confidence and trust in your people. These are essential to sharing responsibility.

7. *Seldom*—One who shares responsibility lets the workers grapple with the problems by themselves as much as possible. Otherwise they quickly become dependent and develop no personal decision-making ability.

8. *No*—This can be a danger sign of a job-centered leader rather than a worker-centered leader. Individual workers should be allowed to set their own pace toward a commonly accepted deadline. How they do it is left to them in shared responsibility.

9. *Always*—If they are asking why, chances are you have created a pleasant climate in which they feel free to question policies and procedures. They feel responsible for what is happening. This is healthy. If you marked seldom, you are probably making too many of the decisions yourself and passing them down under the guise of shared decisions.

10. *Enthusiastically*—People can get excited about a program they believe in and have a part in. Morale is a good indicator of shared responsibility.

If you had 8-10 correct, you are probably skilled in sharing responsibility.

If you had 6-7 correct, you are moving in the right direction.

If you had 5 or fewer correct you are doing too many things yourself and need to begin sharing responsibility with your volunteer workers.

Volunteering to Serve

Christianity is an active religion. Christian churches collect money to spread the gospel, build buildings for education and worship, share the word in the classroom and across the backyard fence. Christianity must be woven into the fabric of our culture, and the volunteer must be a part of this continuing venture.

People want to serve. In our churches are millions of loyal people. They want to be asked to give their allegiance to Christ and his cause. They want to be a part of something with eternal value.

Many times, because the minister is burdened or disappointed in the work of the church, he believes that others feel the same way—that they, too, are low in spirit. The minister's spirit is contagious and becomes a deterrent to healthy challenge and enlistment of the volunteer.

Many church members are highly motivated and encouraged by their own experiences. They hunger to be challenged by their leaders to give their maximum to the kingdom's work.

Can you keep your volunteers?—No other organization or business deals more with people than the church. Churches are in the people business. Most of what the pastor does is for and with his people. He wants to keep them happy in their chosen place of service. To do so he must give attention to his leadership.

The following list indicates how pastors in one survey spend their time. These are ranked according to time spent beginning with the greatest.

1. Sermon preparation and study
2. Pastoral visitation
3. Church administration
4. Preaching/worship leader
5. Evangelistic visitation
6. Education
7. Counseling

Note that in this study education received next to the least amount of time from the pastor. A pastor may avoid the area of education because he feels unprepared to function in that area. He also may see less immediate results in the area of education, or he may not like to function in that area at all. This may indicate the need for an additional staff member whose ministry focuses on education. This will be addressed in the last two chapters of this book.

Churches are built and sustained by the educational organizations of the church. The pastors will retain more of his workers by functioning as an educator to them. As workers become increasingly better trained, the pastor can move on to other areas while the church continues to benefit from worker training. This is a great compliment to a pastor's ministry.

Can the volunteer be motivated?—Volumes have been written on the subject of motivation, and you have probably read many of them. I would like to look at what can be some demotivating factors.

• Amplification of mistakes

As a young boy living in the country, I was riding in the back of the pickup from our country church, Clear Fork Baptist Church. My Dad had told me I would be OK as long as I didn't stand up. Well, I did stand up and fell out and into the gravel, peeling the skin off the side of my face and arm. My grandmother put me in the guest bedroom. Dad came in and, very much out of character, said, "Son, didn't I tell you not to stand up?" His words did not ease my pain. I needed the healing of a kind word from my father. I did not need the amplification of a mistake.

Volunteers will make mistakes and should be allowed to do so. Workers who are continually reminded of what they do wrong will soon avoid taking any action.

• Project not important

We hear about some great project another church has done; and we say we ought to do it, too. The project may contribute little to what our church should be doing. But a minister can become so intoxicated with a project that, regardless of what others think, we will do it. While the project is going on, people ask, "Why are we doing this?" And after it's over, they ask, "What did we gain for all our expenditure of time and money?" Projects should be important to the people who do them.

• Volunteers treated as meaningless

Did you ever have the feeling that someone was asking you questions but not listening to your answers? You don't honor me by asking my opinion if you ignore my response. The leader who manipulates and uses input as an academic exercise will find his creative workers leaving him.

• Conflict among leaders

People want to be led by leaders who are in agreement. Members find it difficult to follow leaders going in different directions. A congregation is proud of its leaders when they work as a team. I am thrilled when I hear a member say, "Our pastor and people work so well together."

Persons' needs, according to Abraham Maslow, are organized in a series of levels—physical, safety, belonging, love, respect, and self-esteem.[1] Church members may or may not respond to a challenge to serve because of their need levels. One person may be so occupied with meeting his family's food and shelter needs that he cannot do anything at church. We must be careful not to condemn him. Another person's social needs are not being met, and she serves because of a hunger just to fellowship with others. When needs on the first three levels are met in the lives of our volunteers, then they are more apt to be happy workers. Healthy volunteers serve because they feel good about themselves and find fulfillment in serving.

A satisfied need is not a motivator. A meal at church may not be a strong motivator, but the fellowship that results may meet an existing need. If people find fulfillment in a good meeting after a meal, they can be highly motivated.

Here are some factors (motives) that motivate volunteers to serve.

• Influence.—"I was challenged to follow the example of another adult."

• Recognition.—"It makes me feel good when someone says, 'He's my Sunday School teacher.' Or, 'You're doing a great job.'"

• Service.—"I want to help others learn about the things of God."

• Worth.—"I want my life to count for something."

• Duty.—"Every Christian should thank the Lord by serving

him in some way."

• Rewards.—"If I help my church, I know good will come to me."

• Fellowship.—"I enjoy working and being with such a nice group of people."

• Mission.—"I love my church work, and it gives meaningful direction to my life."

To study these eight factors and rank them according to which have highest value for you may be an interesting exercise. Many people honestly say that recognition is at the top on their list. Rewards and duty seem to have the least influence on people to serve. As ministers, we need to be aware of why people want to serve. There are other factors such as love and guilt that are not listed. Spend some time thinking about these factors, and consider how you can use this information to improve enlistment and motivation skills.

Enlisting and Reenlisting the Volunteer

The average Southern Baptist church experiences a one-third turnover of volunteer workers each year. Why do so many decline to serve again? Their reasons might help us to improve our enlistment procedures. Much enlistment work each year is really reenlistment. Whether it's a first-time request or reenlistment, these principles should be observed.

Look at people first.—Perhaps you have been guilty as I have. I have watched people join our church and wondered: *Could he teach that men's class? She might be able to help with the Church Training group.* And as I welcomed persons into the fellowship of our church, one of my first questions would be, "What did you do in your previous church?" I'm sure many of them resented my line of questioning.

People want to be challenged to serve, but they want to be dealt with as individuals who have particular needs for their own spiritual growth. How much better to approach a person with their needs in mind rather than our organizational vacancies. When I have pushed people into service, I am more likely to have had a casualty, pushed out of service.

During a seminar for pastors and ministers of education at the Sunday School board, I invited six volunteer workers from local churches to discuss volunteer enlistment. I asked the panel how they felt about the enlistment procedures used by their own church leaders.

The panel replied with comments such as:

"Please don't enlist us in the church hall." They would have preferred being approached in their homes.

"We were not told what was expected of us. They seemed to think we already knew." And none of the volunteers were told that they would be offered training.

Those on the panel said things that church leaders need to hear. Volunteers think these things but rarely tell their leaders.

In a church where I was serving, a man told me he wished he could be head usher. He couldn't because his wife needed him to help her in a preschool class. He helped her, but he didn't enjoy it. In fact, he disliked coming to church. We helped his wife enlist a new teacher, and he became an usher.

Christian service should not be a burden but an opportunity of growth for the volunteer. Dare to ask people what they would really like to do in their church. We need to be sensitive and not force people into empty positions because of our needs but enlist them with their own desires and growth in mind.

Avoid pressure methods.—Church leaders sometimes feel compelled to use pressure methods because they have failed to activate the nominating committee early enough or they have not given needed attention to vacancies. There seems to be a universal, unwritten policy in Southern Baptist churches that on the first Sunday of October all church-elected positions must be filled. This thinking can make us reckless in our enlistment, and we may just enlist other problems.

With proper planning and training of potential workers, we can avoid having to use pressure methods. With training you can have people waiting to serve. This sounds impossible, but

I know it can be true. I have seen it.

As a minister of education, I was often asked to enlist a worker who had not said yes. I guess the nominating committee members thought that surely no one would say no when asked to serve by a staff minister. Every worker should be approached only after the committee has prayed and the enlister can go in the strength of prayer. People should not have to be begged to do God's work. Just as a minister is called, so the volunteer should be called to serve. Ministers did not choose their occupation because no one else would do it, nor do they serve to please others. Likewise a church volunteer should not accept a position just to fill a vacancy or to please the pastor. Church volunteers must respond to a divine invitation to do their work.

Many ministers have become experts at using godly guilt to force a church member into service. People will serve without that kind of manipulation if a need is presented in a healthy, challenging, and honest way. God has proved it over and over again; when he reveals to us a need, he is also through his Holy Spirit preparing someone to respond to that need. People want to be loyal to the cause of Christ; they want to be a part of the mission of the church. They need not be forced to serve by human persuasion.

Use personal contacts.—No one likes to be taken for granted. In my own church last year the nominating committee apparently assumed I would serve again. I wasn't even asked. I felt unappreciated. Time should be taken to visit the potential or reenlisted volunteer at home. This method takes time, but the many rewards are worth the effort. Enlisting volunteers in the minister's office may put them in a position where they do not feel free to express themselves. They have that freedom in their own homes.

The visit should allow ample time for prayer and for an intelligent response to the need presented. Don't expect an answer on the first visit. We honor the work and the person by this approach. Few of us would buy a new car on the phone or through a casual contact on the street. We want to know all we can before we make a major investment. Why should we be so casual and lax about asking an individual to give at least a year of service to a church position?

Share expectations.—There will be expectations, written or unwritten, of those who are elected to church positions. The nominating committee member should know these and share them when first approaching the potential volunteer. If a teacher is expected to tithe, this should be explained before an answer is given. If they are to visit their pupils, this should be shared during the enlistment process.

Some churches have workers' covenants that volunteers are expected to fulfill. A workers' covenant can be a useful tool for enlistment. It can also be used as a reminder later when a worker fails to measure up. Caution should be exercised that the covenant is not used to keep workers in line. The best workers' covenant is the one written by the volunteers themselves. They will be more apt to accept it if they write it.

If expectations were not shared before enlistment, it will be difficult and unfair to attempt to do so later. Many workers have said in all honesty, "I didn't know it would take this much time to be a teacher, or I would never have said yes to the nominating committee." We enlist our problems. Even good enlistment procedures can have disappointments for both the church and the volunteer.

Be fair to the volunteer about a place of service. Don't say, "It's easy; you can do it!" A concerned worker will think, *If it's supposed to be so easy, why is it so difficult for me to do it?* Most volunteer positions in the church are not easy, and they will take time.

Supply needs.—"Here's a quarterly, and I know you have a Bible. That's all you need to work with this group!" As workers become involved in their work, they will discover that their task would be enriched if additional materials were available. It is unfair not to equip workers with needed materials.

An RA leader shared with me that he had to purchase his own materials. This may be demotivating to volunteers because it communicates that their program, their task, or they themselves are unimportant.

I have known teachers who had to beg to get chalkboards for their classrooms. They often bought them and put them up themselves. Why not ask the Sunday School director if any of these kinds of supplies are needed for next year and put them in the budget? It is much easier to say yes if money is allocated for materials.

Training Workers

What do you think about worker training? Have your ideas changed over the years? Have you noticed any change in your ministry as a result of your emphasis on training?

Training is time-consuming. It takes time and money. Is it worth it? The testimony of pastors who have insisted on worker training would be yes!

We spend much effort finding, enlisting, and supplying the volunteer, assuming that somehow they will get trained along the way. Many workers are trained on the job by being placed alongside an experienced worker. This is one good method of training, assuming the seasoned teacher knows and uses good methods and materials.

I have a great auto mechanic. He was good at working on my old Pontiac; but when I took my new Oldsmobile to him, he couldn't do some of the needed repairs. He hadn't received the needed training to service my new car. Even the most experienced workers need continuing training for new ideas, materials, and methods.

Let's look at some questions about training workers. Some of this material has come from a study made by the Research Services Department of the Sunday School Board.[2]

Check your budget.—What percentage of your church budget represents training for your volunteer workers? I have studied the expenditures of churches large and small and found a lack of investment in training. And that's what training is, a good investment. In studying my own church's budget, I found that less than .5 percent is spent for worker training. What return can we expect?

Some small churches have no money allocated for training. For many churches paying the utilities and the preacher and buying literature are musts. Money for training workers is a luxury.

Look at your budget to see what you spent last year. If you spent 2 percent, you are among the highest of Southern Baptist churches. A challenging goal would be 2.5 percent of your total budget. For a budget of $30,000, that would be $750. Is that possible?

Select training events.—How many and what kind of training events do you plan for your church organizations each year? Since training is basic, all churches need to provide worker training. Yet research shows that the smaller the church the less training is provided. Nearly half (47%) of small churches (300 members or less) reported no annual training events.

The best opportunities offered churches large or small are associational training events. Most associations offer a vast amount of free training. The wise pastor can begin by taking his Sunday School or Church Training director along with him to an associational training school. The pastor can easily function here as his own minister of education.

You can also call your association or state office and find many willing workers just waiting for your invitation to come and help. Many of your workers are waiting on you to lead out in the area of training. You can't do it all, but you can act as a broker between your workers and prepared trainers.

Plan your calendar.—Sixty-five percent of small churches plan a calendar of events. As pastor, you can choose from the associational and state training dates and place them on your church calendar. These dates are available at least a year ahead of time. Why not provide a listing of events and dates for your workers each fall. Then promote these training dates a month and a week ahead. Your workers will appreciate the emphasis.

Give recognition.—Recognition is a great motivator. People like to be recognized for their accomplishments. Announce in the services those who have received training. Merited praise will encourage others to get involved. One way to encourage training is through the Church Study Course. This system offers short courses for training leaders and potential leaders in your church. Credit for training can be received through group or individual study. Check your *Baptist Book Store* or *Church Study Course Catalog* for courses available.

Set training goals.—Challenge your workers to move beyond their present training with realistic goals. For example, a goal could be set that 20 percent of your elected Sunday School workers will complete at least one Church Study Course book in their area of work next year. People like to set and reach goals, but they often wait for someone to lead them. Attained goals encourage us to set higher goals. It is exciting to work toward goals, and it is rewarding to reach them.

Working with the Nominating Committee

All church-elected positions should be brought to the church through the nominating committee. Those elected to the committee should have the interest of the total church and show it by their own active involvement. They should seek to enlist the most capable volunteers for all organizations.

Structuring the committee.—Members should be elected to serve a three-year term. The number of members can be a multiple of three (3-6-9), electing one third new members each year. This allows for a continuation of the committee's work history. Members can be selected by the church at large. The committee should not be self-perpetuating, or it could become a power structure.

Planning the work.—The committee should establish its own meeting times which will not take members away from their other places of service. Working ahead with a planned schedule will avoid having to have frequent meetings in September.

I recommend working on levels of responsibility. Select department leaders before moving on to the class or group level.

This is fair and keeps one organization from getting all the choice leaders.

The committee will appreciate worksheets. On the worksheets list across the top of the page: Position, Present Person, This Year's Selection, Contacted By, Decision. You can make your own or purchase from your Baptist Book Store a *Church Nominating Committee Kit* or *Worksheets*.

Divide up the names of adult members who have joined your church in the past year for contact by committee members. Share with new members that you represent the church as a member of the nominating committee and would like to speak with them about how they would like to serve their church. Also contact those who have served in the past; they may again be interested in a place of service. This information can be gathered to assist the committee before actual staffing is started.

Encourage volunteer leaders, especially program and department directors, to commit to extended periods of service. Then encourage them to train to improve their effectiveness. The church should send these persons to Ridgecrest or Glorieta to equip them in their specialized area. They can then share their skills and excitement with others. Even though persons have committed to long-term service, the church will want to elect them annually. This allows for personal and church review of the position and provides a time for reflection, recommitment, affirmation, and support.

To involve as many volunteer leaders as possible, have as a goal that a person have only one major responsibility in the church. This goal will take much prayer and work by the whole church. Increasing your work force and improving your worker training yield results that are worth the labor.

---

[1]Abraham H. Maslow, *Toward a Psychology of Being* (New York: D. Van Norstrand, 1968), p. 25.

[2]J. Clifford Tharp. Jr., "The Pastor Serving as His Own Minister of Education," Research Services Department, Sunday School Board of the Southern Baptist Convention, May 1983.

Going to the post office was a regular part of Brother Loner's daily schedule. His outgoing nature made him enjoy meeting members of his congregation and other persons he had come to know during his service at Hard Rock Baptist Church.

The post office was a good place to catch up on the latest local news and events. It was also Loner's link with the denomination he loved and was, at least most of the time, proud to be a part of. Hardly a day passed that the postal service did not bring him word of some opportunity to increase the effectiveness of his ministry.

Today was no exception. With eagerness Loner tore open that envelope with the familiar Nashville postmark. He could hardly wait to see what was being served by the great denominational cafeteria today.

Sure enough, the fine folk in Nashville were doing it again. They had planned a regional conference especially for pastors just like Loner. They were going to have Dr. Didit, a successful pastor from another state to come and share his testimony of success and achievement. The state denominational leaders from three states all had parts on the program. And T. D. Travelworn, the Sunday School Board's leading authority on the subject, was to be there.

The costs for lodging and conference fees were more than reasonable, and the special rate on travel rounded out the package. No pastor with even a lick of sense would think about missing this event!

Only one flaw marred the otherwise beautiful picture—Brother Loner in his assigned place of service with its post office, one store, two service stations, and fifty-some-odd farm families really didn't need to know, at least presently, how to reach high-rise apartment dwellers.

—George Clark

Chapter 4

Planning Programs and Schedules That Meet Needs

Richard E. Plyler

We are a big denomination. We project big, plan big, act big, think big. We now have fourteen million members in our churches. We are the single largest Protestant denomination in the United States. We have more students enrolled in theological education than any other evangelical denomination in the world. We have the largest missionary force at home and abroad supported financially by any one denomination in the United States.

Though big, we are a denomination made up of many small churches. We have more than twenty-one thousand churches with fewer than three hundred members. Only one church out of nine in our denomination has a minister of education. This means that eight pastors out of nine are responsible for whatever planning, scheduling, and education go on in their churches.

How can we made the educational processes in our churches better? What can those of us who are our own ministers of education do?

We have limited lay volunteers. We may have limited building space for educational programs. We probably have limited teacher and training resources as well as limited financial resources. We also have limited time to give to the educational programs.

The pastor who is the only full-time staff member of a church shoulders a tremendous responsibility and burden.

Ironically, the pastor may be the last to admit that he needs assistance in getting the church's work accomplished. Or he may know of the impossibility of the work but wouldn't dare let anyone know that he knows.

Not too long ago I read a newspaper article by George W. Cornell, a religion writer for the Associated Press, entitled "Stress Hardest on Committed, Idealistic Clergy." Cornell said: "The bigger the expectations, the worse the letdown. That's how experts see the effects on clergy who are shattered by built-up stress. The most idealistic are hit the hardest. Whatever the cause, whether it's increased modern challenges to church life or the temper of the times, the bruising toll of pressures on many clergy has become a widely cited problem. Sometimes it's called 'burnout,' a kind of disillusioned point of despair resulting from accumulated tensions and that often hits those with the highest aims, who care most and try hardest."[1]

A surprise finding of Cornell was what he learned from James Landes, professor of religion at Baylor University. Landes said that the stress level is higher among Southern Baptist ministers than in most denominations. "Our completely autonomous church government structure means all the weight falls on the preacher to keep the churches running."[2] Citing the idealism young ministers bring to their first pastorates, Landes said they need to be prepared for a "lifetime of stress. They need to know how to function when the water hits the wheel."[3]

Pastors often feel they need to be in two or more places at once or doing two or more things at the same time. There is no easy way to be a pastor when it comes to planning programs and church schedules that meet the needs of people, regardless of the demands made on a pastor. It takes work. It takes lots of work.

What has all this to do with my being my own minister of education as far as planning programs and schedules that meet needs? A lot, I believe. There are at least four questions you need to ask yourself as you consider the needs of your church as well as your own personal needs. When these questions are answered adequately, you can begin to plan programs and schedules that effectively meet the needs of your people. The questions are: What do I want my church to accomplish while I am pastor? How can I get the people to help me with my dreams and theirs, and what methods will I use? Do I really know the needs of my people? Am I willing to risk failure?

What Do I Want My Church to Accomplish?

Most of the pastors I know are true visionaries. They dream of good things being done in the churches they serve. They want to accomplish many things for the Lord and for the furtherance of his kingdom on earth. However, sometimes what the pastor is thinking and what the people are thinking may not be the same. Of course, sometimes it is. You have to know where the church you serve has been before you can fully answer the question, What do I want my church to accomplish? Too, you must try realistically to evaluate where you and your church are at the present time in order to know exactly where you want to go with your programs.

Discovering Your Church's History
A church may be only a few months old or celebrating its centennial, but every church has a history. Knowing where your church has been and where it is now will help you project where you want your church to go and how you want to get there.

A good place to begin learning about the history of your church is to do a statistical study of everything reported by the church to the association. Remember that every figure reported means people involvement. Graph your Sunday School enrollment and average weekly attendance over a fifteen- or twenty-year period. You can do this for every organization and special item reported in the minutes. This will take time, but you will learn much about your church. Of course, it will tell you only a part of the story; but it will be enough to see what your church has done.

Another source of information about your church's past is its own minutes. Read these minutes again. You will begin to feel the pulse of your church's past.

Another way to find out about the past of your church is to ask questions of as many members as possible, especially those who have been active the longest. People like to talk about their church. It will also help to ask questions of inactive members and listen to what they say. People in the community who are not members of your church are another good source of information.

As you begin to see the past, you will better understand the present and can see more clearly where the church can and should be in the future. They you can begin to ask what you want your church to accomplish while you are the pastor in terms of programs and schedules that meet people's needs.

Implementing Change

Every new pastor sees changes he wants to make, and he usually gets the changes made but not always with the results he had expected. In one of my pastorates, one of the first things I noticed upon entering the sanctuary was the painting on the back wall of the baptistry. It was one of the most unattractive baptistry paintings I had ever seen. There were no doors or drapes to close off the baptistry when not in use. The thought ran through my mind, *As soon as I can, I'll get permission to close that opening with attractive curtains.*

Several weeks later, as I was reading through the church minutes, I came across an item in one of the business meetings that really caught my attention. This is what I learned: The baptistry painting was accepted as a memorial and was painted by the sister of the deceased. It so happened that the present treasurer of the church was the son of the deceased, and his aunt had painted that picture! You can believe I did not push for changing the baptistry. My back was to it 99 percent of the time anyway!

What do you think would have happened if I had expressed how I felt about the baptistry painting without having that bit of history? I can tell you what did happen. Years later, a new pastor came to this church and decided to close off that awful painting. The ensuing row wounded many church members. The church treasurer and his family and several other families left the church. All of this was so unnecessary. If only the pastor had taken the time to learn about the history of that particular church from a number of sources, including the church's minutes, this situation could have been avoided.

When you have found out where your church has been and what it has accomplished, you can begin to survey and evaluate what is presently being accomplished. Listen to what your people are saying, and continue to ask questions. Jot down ideas you get from members and leaders.

A word of caution—noise alone does not an army make!

It is never wise to listen to just a few people about what they think the church ought to be doing. They may be accurately reporting the pulse of your church family, but it is also possible that they are expressing their own personal opinions about what the church should be doing.

Once there was a farmer who had a pond on his farm. He had spent a number of sleepless nights being kept awake by croaking frogs in his pond. He posted a sign on the side of the highway which read: "Frog Legs For Sale." Soon, a man who owned a restaurant in town stopped by to inquire about the frog legs.

The farmer said, "How many do you want?"

The restaurant owner replied, "How about five hundred?"

The farmer said, "Come back Friday, and they'll be ready."

Friday arrived, and so did the restaurant owner. He said to the farmer, "Have you got my frog legs?"

The farmer replied, "Well, I only have four."

"Only four hundred?" said the restaurant owner.

"No," said the red-faced farmer, "only four frog legs."

The answer is obvious. Two large bullfrogs were making so much noise at night that the farmer assumed his pond must be full of frogs. He didn't check it out first, much to his embarrassment. Even in the smallest churches, you must check out the noise before acting. Preliminary investigation may save you a lot of heartache and disappointment later on.

Surveying Members About Their Dreams

Announce in a morning worship service: "Next Sunday, you will find in your bulletin a sheet of paper with these words: 'I would like to see my church. . . .' During the week, think about what you would like your church to be doing. Next Sunday, you will be given time to complete the sentence. You will be asked to put it in an offering plate when the offering is taken. You will help me and your church leaders as we plan activities and directions for the church."

Make your survey short, so that it can be filled out while the people are sitting in the pew. Get it from them while they are still sitting there. You will get responses. Some of the things suggested will be easily realizable, while other suggestions won't be feasible.

At a later date give out a list of the five things most often mentioned in the survey, and ask members to circle three of the things they would most like to see accomplished. Share this information with your volunteer leaders.

Planning Goals, Not Activities

One rule has helped me in my work as my own minister of education. I believe it can help you, too. *Plan goals, not activities!* Read it again. *Plan goals, not activities.* Generally, this is not the way we plan programs and activity schedules in our churches. We have to be busy doing something all the time, or we feel we aren't doing anything for the Lord and his kingdom. You can be busy and still not accomplish much.

Do you and your church meet just for the sake of meeting? Many do. Is your church still doing the things they did five or twenty-five years ago because it has always been done that way? When you meet, what is the *goal* of your meeting? What do you want to happen or to be accomplished when you meet?

This applies to Sunday School, Church Training, worship, or any other planned meeting or activity.

Some of the questions I ask myself are: "What new thing does the Lord want to do with me and his people? Can what we are doing be improved? If so, how? Do we need to keep doing this; and if so, why? Are we accomplishing the goal we set, if one was set, for this program and/or activity?" Doing activities for the sake of activity will not always meet the needs of your people.

Kennon L. Callahan, in his recent book _Twelve Keys to an Effective Church_, said:

> In this country, the preoccupation of local congregations with programs and activities is deplorable. People win people to Christ; programs do not. People discover people in significant relational groups, not in a merry-go-round of programs and activities. Some churches become so involved in sponsoring a vast array of programs and activities they lose sight of the people those programs and activities allegedly serve. Professional staff become preoccupied with advancing their own territory—the programs and activities related to their arena of responsibility—and lose sight of the people they started out to serve. Increasingly, effective and successful congregations have discovered that people are more important than programs—that people reach other people—precisely because all of us search for groups in which we can discover significant relationships of sharing and caring. Effective congregations offer these groups—and start new groups of similar character in thoughtful, helpful ways.[4]

God is not only a God who creates (activity) but also a God of silence and quiet (even he rested). Many feel that if there isn't something going on at church nothing is being accomplished for God. What we sometimes fail to realize is that God's people are in the world working, living, and playing much more than they are gathering inside the walls of a building set aside for religious purposes. This is not to say that the gathering of God's people isn't important. It is! It may well be the most important event in the lives of his people. But if the people don't know why they are meeting and you don't occasionally remind them of their goals, they may soon feel they have just another meeting to attend. They may choose to stay at home or come and dread the time given.

Often our people are under more stress in their personal lives than we pastors realize. Sometimes we add to that stress by having programs and activities that are almost meaningless because no one remembers the goals for such meetings. When this happens, activities may become more of a burden than the joy intended.

What Methods Should I Use to Get the People to Help?

Showing Appreciation
All human beings have some needs in common. Think of some of your needs. Do you want to be appreciated? Do you have a need to belong? Do you want recognition for your accomplishments? What is your need for affection?

What better place is there for human needs to be met than within a community of caring and loving persons who belong to and know the Lord Jesus Christ? Yet many people who have been active in a local church for years have never had anyone tell them how much their participation and service means to the body of Christ. They plug along for years without any kind of recognition for what they do. What can you do to show sincere appreciation for the service people in your church are rendering to Christ and his kingdom? You can find ways to let them know they are appreciated and are of value to both you and the church.

Twice a year I send a form letter to every person who has been elected to a responsibility in the programs and activities of our church, as well as to many who have volunteered for projects. In this letter are a number of general things I have particularly appreciated. I then take each letter and, using the space left at the bottom front and often the back, I write a personal note. Beginning with the person's name, I write a word of appreciation for what each is doing and has done for our church and our Lord. I make it specific. I want them to know that I know what they do.

Once a year, I publicly recognize everyone who has some kind of responsibility. This is done during morning worship and takes only a few minutes. This is done by groups, by age divisions and program organizations. To recognize one group each Sunday takes about two months. Each worker is recognized. Workers are asked to stand as their names are called and to remain standing until the list is completed. Then everyone gives them a round of applause.

I even recognize those who attend worship only and do not serve in any elected position. I remind them of the importance of their being there Sunday after Sunday. I remind all of us that this is what God has called us to do, to come and worship him because he is worthy to receive our worship. I constantly remind my people that we are not the audience for worship; God is! We are the participators, for we offer our worship to him.

I want our people to know that they are appreciated and that we belong together in working for the Lord and his kingdom. I try to create an atmosphere in which people can motivate themselves to be activly engaged in God's work through a local community of believers.

Our people will participate in programs and activities that meet their needs. It is up to us to find out what those needs are and develop programs and schedules that can best meet those needs.

Sharing Your Dreams

To create an atmosphere in which people can motivate themselves you can become a "seed planter" of ideas which express your visions and dreams for the church family. With one, two, or three persons in your fellowship, you can say, "You know, someday I hope we can. . . ." You can plant seeds of ideas all over the place! Does it really matter who gets credit for the idea if at some time your dream becomes a reality?

It is best not to share your dreams or visions from the pulpit first, especially if they are really new and a radical departure from what has always been done. It is better to plant seeds on a one-to-one basis over a period of time. Then, when the time comes when you do mention it from the pulpit, it will not be such a surprise and won't sound brand new to most. It will be an idea which a number of people have been thinking about over a long period of time.

Too often pastors lay a guilt trip on their people when they present new ideas or their dreams for their church. For example, a pastor gets up one Sunday and says: "I've been praying about a matter for a long time. I firmly believe that it is the Lord's will for us to have a family life building."

For a long time the pastor has been thinking about how nice it would be for his church to have such a facility. There's nothing wrong with that. And he may have been praying about it, too. But this is probably the first time anyone in the church has heard about the idea. They are totally off guard. The people may react positively, but more than likely they will not. Why? Because they haven't had time to think about this idea.

Most people in a service of worship don't get up and disagree with what the pastor is preaching. They can't talk back, argue, or ask questions. How can you argue with "I feel it is the Lord's will for us to have this facility" when it is coming out of the mouth of God's chosen servant?

What often happens is that the pastor takes on the role of prophet when God has called him to be pastor of a certain people, not prophet. Prophets nearly always were unpopular with the people to whom God sent them. If you are going to be a prophet, you must be willing to pay the price.

It is staggering to read, "Forced termination of Southern Baptist ministers is an embarrassment to the denomination, according to Brooks Faulkner, supervisor of the career guidance section at the Sunday School Board."[5] The article continued, "Faulkner estimates, conservatively he thinks, that some 2,500 Southern Baptist church staff ministers are dismissed annually in a dilemma the denomination does not know how to handle."[6]

A question you need to ask yourself is, "What do my people want of me and from me?" From what I have learned and how I see myself, my expectations of me in my role as minister is not always the same as the way my people see me or their expectations of me. I need to know both in order to keep disappointment of expectations to a minimum. I need to let my people know when we aren't on the same wavelength, and adjustments will probably have to be made by both of us.

Including Others in Decision Making
John Naisbitt, in his book _Megatrends_, included a chapter entitled, "From Representative Democracy to Participatory Democracy." He said: "The ethic of participation is spreading bottom up across America and radically altering the way we think people in institutions should be governed. Citizens, workers, and consumers are demanding and getting a greater voice in government, business, and the marketplace. . . . The guiding principle of this participatory democracy is that people must be part of the process of arriving at decisions that affect their lives."[7] He further stated, "People must feel that they have 'ownership' in a decision if they are to support it with any enthusiasm."[8]

Churches are made up of people, all kinds of people. The people in your church and the people in the church three miles down the road may not be alike in their needs and most often are not. Find out what your people want to do and ways they can fulfill their needs. You won't have a lot of trouble getting done the things they really want to do.

For years I tried to interest our people in having missions education organizations for children and youth. I got nowhere. So I finally quit struggling with the idea. Four years passed, and one day a woman said to me, "You know, Pastor, I wish we had GAs."

I replied: "Why don't you talk with some other mothers and see how they feel about it. If there is enough interest, maybe you and some others could receive some training; and we could get the girls organized." In less than three years we had not only an active GA group but also Mission Friends, Acteens, and Crusader and Pioneer RAs. When some of the people decided we needed missions education organizations, we got them! I had to be listening. You will, too!

Do I Really Know the Needs of My People?

Discovering Members' Needs

To find out what some of the needs of your people are, you are going to have to do some research. What are the ages of your church family? How many widows/widowers are there? How many single persons are there, and what are their ages? How many children are there? What ages? To whom do these children belong? How many youth are there? How many college students are there? How many are in the military? How many are newly married or trying to get established in careers? How many people are within five years of retirement? How many are already retired?

How many people in your church family have traveled more than two hundred miles from where they now live? How many persons would be considered newcomers? How many clusters of kinfolk do you have in your church family? Where are your people employed? What is the average income for the families in your church? Within the past five years how many family units have experienced some kind of crisis or grief experience? What kind of health-related problems do your people have? What are they doing about them?

Who attends what and when? What physical resources do you have for worship, educational programs, and other related activities? Are there needs in these areas? Do the people feel the same about this as you do?

Is the power structure in your church visible, invisible, or a combination? Is the power structure basically good or bad? Is there a power struggle taking place at the present time and, if so, between whom? What are the causes?

What is the educational level of your adult members? How would you rate the emotional maturity of your youth and adults?

We could go on and on with viable questions that need to be asked if you are going to discover the needs of your people. Answering these questions will take time and effort, but it will be well worth it.

Understanding Your Own Needs

Learn all you can about yourself, what your needs are, and how these needs continue to change. As you also learn what the needs of your people are, you can begin to lead your church to meet those needs if it is at all possible. As legitimate as the need or needs may be, it may not be possible for you or the church to meet them.

There are some things you will probably never accomplish no matter how long you stay in one pastorate. You have to look at your expectations and seek ways to fulfill them. Too, you may at times have to lower your expectations in order not to be disappointed. Ministers are sometimes too idealistic for their own good.

Are You Willing to Fail?

No one wants to be a failure, ministers least of all. However, being human beings, we are bound to fail. No one is perfect. With the cultural emphasis on success and the church emphasis on growth, we don't want to think about failure.

Failure happens to the best of us. How we handle success, as well as failure, will determine how effective our leadership is going to be. If we expect always to be successful, we are going to be terribly disappointed at some point in our pilgrimage as a pastor. We had better learn how to recognize failure and how to deal with it. If we are unable to do this, we will be prone to depression and low self-esteem. We will work harder but not smarter. We will ignore the obvious (failure) and pray harder for the Lord to turn stones into bread (success). We will have to deal with anger; and more often than not, we will become angry preachers in our pulpits.

When is the last time you and your church tried something that failed and you, or someone else, got up and said, "Well, it looks like we failed with this (project, program, or whatever)"? Or are we more like the subjects of the fabled emperor who walked around naked while his subjects pretended he was fully clothed (and the emperor believed he was)? Sometimes what we attempt just won't work. It may later, but now now. We work, plan, implement, and sometimes fail; but we will hardly admit when something isn't working. We don't handle failure well. We have tried to remove completely the word *failure* from our vocabulary. Try as we may, it is still in the dictionary!

Are you willing to fail and admit it? Have you, as a pastor, ever gone to your weekly or monthly pastors' conference and heard some pastor get up and tell about his failures since the last meeting? Hardly! What you will hear is the glowing reports of "yesterday" (Sunday) and all the marvelous ways the Lord did bless. It may be true that the Lord did bless; but how much more healthy, emotionally and spiritually, it would be to admit failure when it happens. And it does happen! Are you willing to risk failure in planning programs and schedules? Be honest with yourself and take it from there for personal growth.

Since no two churches are alike and no two pastors are alike, needs will differ. In trying to learn how to plan programs and schedules that meet needs, ask these questions: (1) What do I want this church to accomplish while I am pastor? (2) How can I get the people to help me with my dreams as well as their own, and what methods will I use? (3) Do I really know the needs of my people and myself? (4) Am I willing to risk failure in planning programs and schedules? Your journey will be easier if you will *plan goals, not activities!*

Have joy in your journey!

[1]George W. Cornell, "Stress Hardest on Committed, Idealistic Clergy," *The Gastonia Gazette* (Feb. 4, 1984), p. 6.
[2]Ibid.
[3]Ibid.
[4]Kennon L. Callahan, *Twelve Keys to an Effective Church* (San Francisco: Harper & Row, 1983), p. 39.
[5]Jim Lowry, "Dilemma Embarrasses SBC," *Facts & Trends*, 28, No. 2 (February 1984), p. 10.
[6]Ibid.
[7]John Naisbitt, *Megatrends* (New York: Warner Books, 1982), p. 59.
[8]Ibid., p. 188.

"Brother Loner, I heard the most wonderful sermon!" announced Mrs. Pewworn.

"Well, that's certainly very kind of you. It was good perhaps but hardly wonderful."

"Oh, no! I was talking about a sermon I heard last week while I was visiting my sister. They were having a revival at their church, and I went one night. Have you ever heard Brother Wringer?"

"No, I can't remember having heard that name before. Is he good?"

"Is he good? I'll tell you, Pastor, I've never heard a preacher who would compare with him." Brother Loner only hoped his countenance did not betray the hurt and anger he felt rising up within him. "He had such power. Why, his voice rattled windows at the back of the auditorium."

"He projected well then?"

"Oh, I'll say he did. And he just made you *feel* something. If he'd given an invitation for mission service, I'd have bought a ticket to China or somewhere."

"I can tell you enjoyed his message. What did he preach about?"

"Well, his text was from. . . . He talked about. . . . Brother Loner, I'm embarrassed. I can't remember a thing he had to say. But I'll never forget hearing him preach! It's just not every day you get a chance to hear preaching like that. I just hope we can have him for a revival sometime."

—George Clark

Chapter 5

Pastor as Preacher/Teacher

James E. Hightower, Jr.

Jesus, the Model Teacher

J. A. Marquis said: "Teaching was his [Jesus'] chief business. He was often a healer, sometimes a worker of miracles, frequently a preacher, but always a teacher."[1]

While this sounds good, we must admit that Jesus saw himself as the Son of man with all that the term implies. He is judge; he is returning; he is human. Jesus is the model teacher; but he claims a broader base for his ministry, that of the Son of man.

However, his disciples and those around him definitely saw him as a teacher. No passage of Scripture is more representative of Jesus than Luke 13:22. "He went on his way through towns and villages, teaching, and journeying toward Jerusalem" (RSV).[2] Even more importantly his opponents viewed him as a teacher. Mark 12:14 shows a group of Pharisees coming to him saying: "Teacher, we know that you are true, and care for no man; for you do not regard the position of men, but truly teach the way of God. Is it lawful to pay taxes to Caesar, or not?" (RSV).

The Gospels record instances of Jesus' teaching his disciples privately. They also recount Jesus' teaching large crowds in public places. One instance of this is Matthew 5—7, the section of Scripture we normally refer to as the Sermon on the Mount. The clear intent of this section of Scripture is to teach,

71

so it is really Jesus' Teaching on the Mount.

Apparently Jesus was acknowledged as an ordained rabbi. He was consulted on ethical matters such as when it was lawful to divorce. He was also asked about family conduct. The following instance of a family quarrel is indicative of this. "One of the multitude said to him, 'Teacher, bid my brother divide the inheritance with me.' But he said to him, 'Man, who made me a judge or divider over you?' And he said to them, 'Take heed, and beware of all covetousness; for a man's life does not consist in the abundance of his possessions'" (Luke 12:13-15, RSV).

Jesus was also asked about theological issues. Questions such as, How many will be saved? were answered by Jesus. The passage from Luke 13:23-24 is illustrative of this. "And some one said to him, 'Lord, will those who are saved be few?' And he said to them, 'Strive to enter by the narrow door; for many, I tell you, will seek to enter and will not be able'" (RSV).

To say that Jesus was acknowledged as a rabbi does not mean he was popular. For example, in the synagogue at Capernaum, he astonished the people. Jesus' teaching and healing ministry were also connected. Often, when Jesus was asked to display his power, he was addressed simply as, "Teacher." "Teacher, do you not care if we perish?" (Mark 4:38, RSV). "And one of the crowd answered him, 'Teacher, I brought my son to you, for he has a dumb spirit'" (Mark 9:17, RSV).

Although Jesus cast his ministry in the larger frame of Son of man, he was known by friends and foes alike as "teacher."

What Did Jesus Teach?
Jesus had specific aims in mind as he taught persons. They were theological, relational, and ethical.

Jesus taught persons how to be rightly related to God.—I believe it is safe to say that until persons are rightly related to God they cannot know all there is to know about ethics or relationships. Ethics evolve from a right relationship to God.

The same is true in our relationships. When we are related to Jesus Christ as a brother or sister, then we can relate to others as our kin.

Luke 13:3 records Jesus' saying to persons, "Unless you repent you will all likewise perish" (RSV). In the Sermon on the Mount Jesus called for persons to be rightly related to God: "But seek first his kingdom and his righteousness, and all these things shall be yours as well" (Matt. 6:33, RSV).

Jesus taught persons how to be rightly related to others.— Jesus was asked what the most important commandment is. He replied: "The first is, 'Hear O Israel: The Lord our God, the Lord is one; and you shall love your God with all your heart, and with all your soul, and with all your mind, and with all your strength.' The second is this, 'You shall love your neighbor as yourself.' There is no other commandment greater than these" (Mark 12:29-31, RSV). If right relationship to God is important, right relationship to others is also.

I am reminded of a story that illustrates this point superbly.

A few years ago this headline appeared in the Fort Worth _Star Telegram_: "Man, 105, to Be Tried for Killing." The story was about Ed "Possum Slim" Myers, a 105-year-old man accused of killing one friend and wounding another. It seems that Myers and a friend made an agreement to exchange gifts on their birthdays. When Myers went to her home to give her a birthday present of $5 and a half-pint of gin, she wasn't satisfied and grabbed several other bills from his hand. Myers went home, got a pistol, and returned to his friend's. He killed his woman friend and another friend was seriously wounded.

Myers said "righteous anger" caused him to shoot. Then he added that he holds no hard feelings toward her. "Being a church member. I couldn't have no hard heart for her," he said. "That wouldn't be living right."[3]

Jesus gave us a new way of relating to one another. It is the way of self-giving love. Jesus taught this way in both example and deed.

Jesus taught people a new ethic.—Jesus was a master of the

Scripture. That is where any preacher/teacher should begin. Jesus knew that one's life must be built on a foundation. He obviously chose the Scripture as his foundation.

When Jesus was confronted by Satan in the wilderness, he took Scripture as his refuge. In the same manner his teaching and preaching is filled with Old Testament quotations.

The Teaching on the Mount is Jesus' collection of what makes a kingdom citizen. These sayings remind us again that anger is more harmful to us than to the person with whom we are angry. They teach us about the danger of pride. They teach us the all-inclusive nature of love.

Jesus said, "You have heard it said, but I say to you. . . ."

Jesus, the model teacher, taught right relationship to others and a new ethic.

Whom Did Jesus Teach?

Pastors often believe their job is to teach adults. We interpret Ephesians 4:12, "for the equipment of the saints, for the work of the ministry, for building up the body of Christ" (RSV), as if this were our sole teaching function.

When we look at the life of Jesus, we see another model. One time in Jesus' hurried schedule, the disciples forbade the children to come to him. Yet Jesus said, "Forbid them not: for of such is the kingdom of God" (Luke 18:16). Jesus taught the children a lesson that day of what God is like. God always welcomes persons regardless of their size. More than this, however, he taught the disciples and that unnamed crowd a theological lesson.

Jesus was also willing to teach women. Women did not have the status in Jesus' day that they do now. On more than one occasion Jesus had a one-on-one teaching session with a woman. Remember the woman at the well?

Remember Martha after Lazarus' death? "Lord, if you had been here, my brother would not have died" (John 11:21, RSV). Jesus said to her in verses 25-26: "I am the resurrection and the life; he who believes in me, though he die, yet shall he live, and whoever lives and believes in me shall never die.

Do you believe this?"

Jesus taught the woman, as the crowd gathered to stone her, who was caught in the act of immoral sex. Jesus found a cheat like Zacchaeus and believed he was worth teaching. Jesus found a government official like Matthew and believed he could come into right relationship with God. Jesus taught a learned man like Nicodemus in the first Christian night school. Jesus taught the wealthy, the poor, the learned, the ignorant, the minorities of women and children, outcast persons who worked for Rome. Even Jesus' disciples were a mixed lot of humanity.

Church growth theorists are telling us that churches grow in homogeneous groups. This may be true, but Jesus grew the early church with anyone who would listen to him teach.

Jesus was and is the Master Teacher because he embodied the truth, had the needed message, and believed all persons were worth the effort.

The Pastor as an Informal Teacher

How the pastor views education will set the overall tone for how he views himself as teacher.

For example, we have often mistakenly labeled training as education in our churches. We have assumed that if we indoctrinate people to think the way "real Christians" should think then we have taught and they have been educated. Nothing could be further from the truth. The purpose of Christian education is not to produce stagnant persons who have all the right answers to all the questions. Rather, it is to produce growing persons who are obedient to the living Word, Jesus Christ.

Pastors are to be Christian educators who produce growing people, not trainers who produce people with right answers to every problem. There are more trained than educated Christians.

But how does the pastor truly educate persons so that they become godly, growing Christians?

Reveal yourself to the learner.—The day has passed of the pastor's being on the pedestal with the church member below. This self-disclosure of oneself to others will be the basis of being a true educator.

Sidney M. Jourard captured this truth when he said:

We are said to be a society dedicated to the pursuit of truth. Yet, disclosure of the truth, the truth of one's being, is often penalized. Impossible concepts of how man ought to be—which are often handed down from the pulpit—make man so ashamed of his true being that he feels obliged to seem different, if for no other reason than to protect his job. Yet, when a man does not acknowledge to himself who, what, and how he is, he is out of touch with reality, and he will sicken. No one can help him without access to the facts. And it seems to be another fact that *no man can come to know himself except as an outcome of disclosing himself to another person.* This is the lesson we have learned in the field of psychotherapy. When a person has been able to disclose himself utterly to another person, he learns how to increase his contact with his real self, and he may then be better able to direct his destiny on the basis of this knowledge.[4]

Use dialogue instead of monologue.—But how is this accomplished in the art of sermon making?

• Preaching should help persons formulate their own convictions, not formulate convictions for them.

• We should bring the questions, doubts, and affirmations of persons to the preaching task. This can only be done by listening to persons during the week.

• The pastor can ask others' assistance in preparing for the preaching task. Through study groups or worship committees preaching can become inclusive rather than exclusive.

• The pastor might check words he is using in next Sunday's sermons with a small group to see if the words are understandable. Jesus often used far more symbols in teaching/preaching than complex words. We should follow his model.

• The pastor will make an effort to meet people's needs.

These are merely suggestions of how preaching begins to be

dialogical. This list is suggestive, not exhaustive.

An environment that is conducive to effective education will be dialogical rather than monological. Reuel Howe said: "But dialogue can restore a dead relationship. Indeed this is the miracle of dialogue: it can bring relationship into being, and it can bring into being once again a relationship that has died."[5]

Extending your boundaries as a person.—The informal, dialogical teacher will be a growing person.

Jourard expressed it in these terms:

> In the general scheme of things, what consequences follow when men disclose their real selves, one to the other? Here are some of the obvious outcomes:
>
> —They learn the extent to which they are similar, one to the other, and the extent to which they differ from one another in thoughts, feelings, hopes, reactions to the past, etc.
>
> —They learn of the other man's needs, enabling them to help him or to ensure that his needs will not be met.
>
> —They learn the extent to which this man accords with or deviates from moral and ethical standards.
>
> Why do we disclose ourselves, and why do we not? Answers to this question are of enormous importance, since mutual ignorance seems to be at the root of all problems between family members or between citizens of different nations.
>
> Researches I have conducted show that a person will permit himself to be known when he believes his audience is a man of goodwill. Self-disclosure follows an attitude of love and trust. If I love someone, not only do I strive to know him; I *also display my love by letting him know me.* At the same time, by so doing, I permit him to love me.[6]

Notice that a former psychology professor at a major university discusses pivotal Christian issues—love and trust. How do you give or receive love and trust? By being vulnerable to others. Isn't this what God did? He gave his Son who become vulnerable, even to death on a cross.

The pastor is called on to disclose the kind of person he is. This vulnerability is a chief teaching device.

The Pastor as Formal Teacher

Church members need to see their pastor's commitment to teaching. This needs to be a formal commitment on the pastor's part. "I chose to be a teacher." Remember the quote from J. A. Marquis: "Teaching was his [Jesus'] chief business. He was often a healer, sometimes a worker of miracles, frequently a preacher, but always a teacher."[7]

The contemporary pastor has many roles from which to choose. You may perceive yourself to be administrator, business executive, scholar, counselor, preacher, or a host of other roles. But regardless of the role you choose, you are always a teacher. If this is so, why not make it a conscious choice?

Let me suggest ways you can become a teacher.

First, be a teacher of teachers.—Weekly workers' meetings are a time-honored and proved method. Begin being a teacher by meeting weekly with your Sunday School teachers. Let them hear you explain and apply the upcoming week's lesson.

Second, use a variety of teaching methods.—In your weekly workers' meeting do more than explain the Scripture. Model a range of methods teachers can use in teaching. Teachers should not parrot on Sunday morning what the pastor said on Wednesday night. The wise pastor will spend as much time on method as he does on content.

Methods such as discussion, stories, question and answer, drama, role playing, previous assignment, and interviews can add new life to otherwise dull teaching. As you are willing to go beyond lecture to other methods, teachers can find new excitement in teaching.

Let me add a word of caution. Do not abandon the lecture as a bad form of teaching. At times it is the best form for communicating what you are saying. Measure any teaching by what Robert E. Bingham calls the three C's. (1) "It is clear? Can the least mature member of the class understand?" (2) "Is it concise?" If verbosity or unclear symbols cloud your teaching, delete them. (3) "Is it channeled? Does my message strike at the heart of what is being conveyed in this lesson."[8] Never use another teaching method just to be clever.

Third, use your study for Wednesday night teacher training to build Sunday's sermon.—Teachers will be pleased to hear you deal with the same biblical material in worship that they dealt with in Sunday School. This practice makes good use of your time and increases the listening span of your audience.

John Killinger said, "The feeling of unity and progress, when the pulpit and the teacher's lectern are in benevolent and harmonious relationship, with one challenging and feeding the other, belongs to any people of God."[9]

Preaching on the Sunday School text can develop an interplay between the sermon and education that is not possible any other way.

Fourth, take your teachers to training events.—Go as a participant, not as the bus driver. When teachers see your need for learning and your sacrifice of time, they will feel a new sense of commitment.

Training events are offered regularly on the associational, state, and national levels. Each summer Ridgecrest and Glorieta Conference Centers are filled with training opportunities. Find these training opportunities and use them.

Fifth, the pastor should maintain regular contact with the Sunday School and Church Training directors.—Having lunch with these persons every week will help you to stay on the cutting edge of your church's educational ministry.

The pastor, through his personhood, is an informal teacher. The pastor, through modeling the teaching process, is a formal teacher.

Preaching That Enhances the Teaching Ministry

John Killinger declared, "A good sermon is a prime teaching device at the same time that it is a proclamation; and a good lesson inevitably ends by making the gospel more real and visible in the lives of the students."[10]

The proclamation of the gospel through a sermon is a teaching device, but teaching has not truly taken place unless learning occurs. Therefore, we are left with the question, What is learning? Thomas Clayton defined it this way:

> To learn is to engage in an experience that affects the psychological functioning of the individual in ways that will result in changes in his behavior. The word "learning" is used to refer to both the process and the result. As a process, learning refers to the experiences the learner goes through, his internal and external activity, and his reactions to the situation in which he finds himself. As a product, learning refers to the changes that occur, the ways in which the learner is different or the actual change in his behavior. These changes may be temporary or relatively permanent.[11]

So preaching that is teaching leads the hearer to temporary or permanent change.

The confusion between preaching and teaching is as old as the church itself. Very early the church made a distinction between preaching *(kerygma)* and teaching *(didache)*. Preaching was the proclamation of Christianity to non-Christians. Teaching was ethical instruction or interpretation of doctrines to persons interested in Christianity. In fact, most preaching today would not be considered preaching by the early church. Instead it would be the informal discussion of the Christian life to a congregation that is already established. This form of communication was called *homilia* from which our word *homily* is formed.

It seems to me that this is too fine a distinction. *Kerygma, didache*, and *homilia* are all teaching. The early church did not "teach" Jesus Christ; they proclaimed him. Yet, that proclamation was teaching the world about Jesus. Likewise, when Jesus was taught to the early church, that teaching became a proclamation of him as the Son of God. It is not *either* preaching or teaching; it is *both* preaching and teaching. They happen simultaneously.

The Sermon Itself
Ilion Jones said, "Preachers are partners with God in his con-

tinuing redemptive activity, sharers of God's responsibility for the salvation of the world."[12]

The sermon, therefore, is a special teaching tool that both proclaims Jesus to unbelievers and teaches believers about him. God in his wisdom made persons the conveyer of this message. Read what Jones said about the preacher:

> How can the fullness of what God means to human beings be brought more clearly to a group of people than through another human being? A man with mind, conscience, moral judgment, and will; a man who can love, embody virtues in his character, be sensitive to moral values, and be moved with passion for social ideals; a man who can respond to truth, beauty, and goodness, whose personality is aglow with the Spirit of God—such a man is the highest symbol of God known.[13]

The sermon can never be separated from the messenger.

Once the proclaimer sees that the task of preaching Jesus Christ leads persons to change their behavior, the form of the sermon should be examined. Sermons can be divided into at least six classifications:

Exposition.—A systematic study of some portion of Scripture.

Doctrinal.—An interpretation and application of a Christian doctrine such as the fall, the church, or salvation.

Ethical.—Helps for Christians in conducting their daily affairs in light of Christian faith, including topics such as war and peace or family life.

Apologetic.—A philosophical approach to Christian faith to help Christians give an answer for the hope that is in them.

Topical.—An interpretation and application of Christian faith in the light of a current play, movie, or novel.

Evangelistic.—A call for persons to make a decision for Jesus Christ.

One flaw of many good sermons is that they have too many aims. Ordinarily, a sermon should have one purpose. Learning is not enhanced by a shotgun approach to teaching/preaching.

What Makes a Teachable Sermon?

The logical conclusion of this chapter is to identify those elements that make a sermon both teachable and preachable. I have identified six characteristics of the teachable sermon.

First, a sermon is teachable when the preacher is perceived as being a real human being.—A significant part of any sermon is the sermon deliverer.

When the preacher is willing to share his humanity, his message will be believable. When the pastor must act like a plastic saint, his message will not be believable. The preacher must give evidence that he, too, is teachable.

Second, a sermon is teachable when it answers questions people are asking.—The sermon should be grounded in Scripture but originated from human need. The sermon should reveal understanding of human need.

When the preacher is a real person, speaking to a real need, the platform is set for a face-to-face encounter with God!

Third, a sermon is teachable if it has given the congregation a chance to participate.—Remember that persons learn through activity? It's true! Begin a Bible study group that helps you gain insight from the Scripture. Start a worship committee that aids in planning, implementing, and evaluating worship. Use deacons and other lay leaders in the worship event. People learn best through activity, not passivity.

Fourth, a sermon is teachable when it appeals to as many of the senses as possible.—One of the beauties of observing the Lord's Supper is that it can appeal to all five senses.

The traditional sermon appeals to one sense (hearing) and very limitedly to sight. Each sense the pastor can add to the sermon makes it more teachable.

Fifth, a sermon is teachable that builds on past experience.—At times the wise pastor will lay extensive groundwork before preaching on a given issue. If a church has been plagued by conflict, the pastor will need to spend much time in relationship building, listening, and interpreting before publicly confronting the issue in a sermon.

Previous situations in an individual's or a community's life will affect learning. The wise pastor uses this to good advantage for the kingdom's sake.

Sixth, a sermon is teachable when it helps persons meet their needs for security, mastery, and belonging.—Security will help persons build their self-esteem and affirm their worth in God's sight. Mastery will help persons see their lives in such a way that they are free to choose for or against God. Belonging will affirm the sense of community found in the local church. Belonging needs will also be met as the invitation is extended to join this household of faith.

Teaching is not complete until a new awareness of truth has broken through or until behavior has been temporarily or permanently changed. Preaching that is teachable must be directed at enhancing a person's or community's knowledge or changing their behavior in the light of Jesus Christ.

Then a pastor can truly be the teacher and the preacher.

[1]John A. Marquis, *Learning to Teach from the Master Teacher* (Philadelphia: Westminster Press, 1918), pp. 76-77.

[2]From the Revised Standard Version of the Bible, copyrighted 1946, 1952, © 1971, 1973. Subsequent quotations are marked RSV.

[3]Steve Wallace, "Conduct," *Proclaim*, 12, No. 1 (October 1981), p. 33.

[4]Sidney M. Jourard, *The Transparent Self* (New York: D. Van Nostrand, 1971), p. 6.

[5]Reuel L. Howe, *The Miracle of Dialogue* (New York: Seabury Press, 1963), p. 3.

[6]Jourard, p. 5.

[7]Marquis, pp. 76-77.

[8]Robert E. Bingham, *New Ways of Teaching the Old Story* (Nashville: Broadman, 1970), p. 48.

[9]John Killinger, *The Centrality of Preaching in the Total Task of the Ministry* (Waco: Word Books, 1969), p. 86.

[10]Ibid., pp. 80-81.

[11]Thomas E. Clayton, *Teaching and Learning, a Psychological Perspective* (Englewood Cliffs, New Jersey: Prentice-Hall, 1965), p. 35.

[12]Ilion T. Jones, *Principles and Practice of Preaching* (Nashville: Abingdon, 1979) p. 20.

[13]Ibid., p. 23.

Brother Loner stopped at the top of the church steps, took out his handkerchief and mopped his brow, and pulled up his pants. Getting that church literature out of the back of his car and up to the church office got to be a bigger job every quarter. At least the packages were easier to unwrap now that they were wrapped in plastic. Loner still had a few scars from back in the old days when the literature was wrapped in brown paper and tied with copper wire.

One thing that hadn't gotten any easier was trying to remember which age youngsters got which quarterlies. Did *Bible Searchers* go to the older ones or the younger ones? Who got *Bible Discoverers*? There didn't seem to be any *Builders*. Had that bunch in Nashville messed up the order again?

Loner longed for the days of beginners and primaries and juniors and such. He had never quite got over all the changes. Things seemed to be more simple before. If only he had someone who could keep up with things like that and be aware of the latest trends in religious education. The church needed a minister of education, but it would be years before they could afford one.

"Hello, Dear. Did we get our *Open Windows*?" Mrs. Loner asked.

"Yes, I think I saw some. I'm glad you're here. Can you straighten this mess out? You know this stuff better than I do. You must have stayed awake during our seminary RE classes."

—George Clark

Chapter 6

Pastor's Wife as Minister of Education

Charlotte Bowles Baker

Mary enjoys working with people. She recognizes the value of religious education. She is a planner and an organizer. Even if she were not the pastor's wife, she would be actively involved in the church. Mary is a prime candidate to serve as a minister of education in the church her husband pastors.

Many pastors' wives have the qualifications to serve as minister of education if given the opportunity to do so. Numerous churches depend on their pastors for leadership in religious education. These churches could be enriched by availing themselves of the talents of their pastors' wives. Pastors would profit from the tremendous help of their wives.

Unique Role

The pastor's wife who accepts the responsibility of minister of education walks into a unique situation. Her relationship with church members takes on an added dimension. She and her husband now have a professional relationship. The community views her in a different light.

Pastors' wives have not traditionally served in staff positions. In Southern Baptist churches ministers of education are usually male. This means that she is in a doubly unique role by being both a pastor's wife and female. Few role models exist on either count. But the uniqueness of the situation should not hinder a pastor's wife from serving as minister of education. A pastor's wife called to this position can be an asset to her husband's ministry. It is a ministry which is personally rewarding and leads to the spiritual growth of individuals in the church.

The pastor's wife who accepts a staff position is on the cutting edge of new vistas of service for women. Women have comprised the volunteer force of churches for years. They have primarily been the educators in our churches. The time has come for women to be leaders in a professional sense. Women such as Deborah, Lydia, Priscilla, and Phoebe set the precedent for women in ministry. God calls women as well as men into his service. As Southern Baptists, we are just beginning to recognize the potential for women dedicated to serving God. Jesus raised the status of women in his day, thereby changing the place of women for all time. The Holy Spirit was sent to lead us into all truth. We have been slow to accept the truth that God can use females as well as males. But doors of opportunity are opening. One of those opportunities is for the pastor's wife to serve as minister of education.

Lacking role models, the pastor's wife has a degree of freedom she might not otherwise experience. She is less restricted by preconceived notions of what is expected of her. Often this is a church's first experience with a minister of education. They are grateful for the ministry of their pastor's wife.

Two areas of difficulty may be encountered by women in ministry, "those caused by their own unrealistic expectations and those caused by the sexist reactions of others."[1] Any new person, male or female, on the field will encounter a period of scrutiny. Viewing this period as normal will ease the feelings of sexism. Dianne Kessler stated that "the greatest source of strength for a woman in a leadership role should come from confidence based upon competence."[2] Competent service with genuine love for God and the congregation will lead to acceptance. Feelings of anxiety and uncertainty may accompany the pastor's wife who assumes the position of minister of education. These feelings are a normal part of any new endeavor. The pastor's wife will find herself on occasion the only woman in a meeting. Her attitudes of professionalism and self-confidence will put the men at ease.

The pastor's wife's whole attitude about serving as minister of education is critical to her success as a religious educator. Being the pastor's wife may mean that the congregation expects more of her. Her spirit of devotion to God and a desire to further his kingdom enable her to meet this challenging opportunity.

Volunteer Versus Paid

Should the pastor's wife be paid for her services as a minister of education? Many dynamics enter into the decision to pay the pastor's wife. Churches differ in their attitudes. Some churches frown on the pastor's wife serving in a position with a title, much less paying her. Other churches are delighted for their pastor's wife to serve, even being willing to pay her. Pastors' wives approach service from different perspectives. Some pastors' wives will serve anywhere there is a need with or without pay. Other pastors' wives will give only a tenth of their time without pay.

There are advantages and disadvantages to being a volunteer or being paid. The volunteer can set her own hours of work to fit the demands of her varied roles. She can do as much or as little educational work as she desires. She is responsible to no one any more than any other volunteer in the church.

The volunteer minister of education can determine her own job description to a large degree. Most churches are accustomed to their pastor's leading the educational program. They may not be aware of the varied dimensions of educational work. The pastor's wife in this role can show the church the benefits of an educational ministry.

The pastor's wife may serve in a volunteer position when the church would not consider paying her. If she can view this as an opportunity for Christian service, she can experience a fulfilling ministry.

There also may be disadvantages to serving as a volunteer

minister of education. For the seminary-educated pastor's wife especially, there is the potential for a diminished self-image. The time and money spent in receiving an education are largely ignored. She often views the church as wanting all they can get without having to pay.

Churches generally employ a minister of music long before they recognize the need for a minister of education. Often the minister of music does not have formal education in the music ministry, much less a degree in music. A situation such as this tends to increase the feelings of low self-esteem. A pastor's wife in such a position will have to reconcile for herself what she can handle. Some wives will feel comfortable serving without pay. They serve with the realization that to whom much is given much is required. Others will not be able to accept the responsibilities without pay. They believe the church has an ethical responsibility to pay for qualified leadership.

There are advantages to being paid as a minister of education. The most obvious is that the pastor's wife is seen as a professional. The church recognizes her expertise. Members accept their ethical responsibility to pay for the knowledge her education has produced. The hours she spends in directing the educational program of the church deserve remuneration.

The self-esteem of the pastor's wife blossoms when the church compensates her for her service. This may lead to a more productive ministry. The paid pastor's wife may realize more authority to do the work she sets out to accomplish.

Too often churches have the attitude of, "Let's get two for the price of one." A question frequently asked by pulpit committees is, "What does your wife do?" Paying a qualified pastor's wife can create good will between the minister's family and the church.

There are also disadvantages to the pastor's wife being paid as minister of education. The first disadvantage is the unfavorable attitude of church members. Many members think their pastor's wife is a wonderful person because she does so much church work. If she were paid, some people would question her motives. Paying the pastor's wife could cause division in the church.

Second, the paid pastor's wife will have set hours, a job description, and perhaps a supervisor. With the authority achieved by salary comes accountability to the church.

Third, the church tends to expect perfection from the pastor's wife once she is employed. One pastor's wife put it this way: "If you are a volunteer, many demands cannot be made of you. If you are paid, it seems they want 100 percent perfection."

Finally, the church may feel that they can employ the pastor's wife cheaper than an outside person. This attitude has the potential for creating ill will, but it does not have to do so.

The church may have to be shown the benefits of having a minister of education. This may mean starting out as a volunteer with or without the goal of being paid. The church may soon realize that the pastor's wife deserves a salary, but they may believe that they cannot afford to pay a respectable salary for another staff member. Recognizing a moral responsibility to pay should lead the church to pay something. Some pastors' wives would gladly accept a smaller salary as opposed to no salary.

Ideally, the pastor's wife with a seminary education will receive a salary. Realistically, churches are not always as progressive in their attitudes as they should be. The seminary-trained, as well as other pastor's wives, may have to begin as volunteers. For some the day may come when they will move from volunteer to paid positions.

The transition from volunteer to part-time will probably involve work with the personnel committee. The pastor's wife should prepare a time study for several months showing the time she spends on the education ministry. She will probably be asked to give some guidelines for a job description. The difference between an educational secretary and a minister of education may need to be explained.

This transition should be approached with care. What the

pastor's wife does not only affects her, but it also affects her husband's ministry. A spirit of unity in the church should exist if this change takes place.

Preparation for Leading the Educational Program

Certain traits are genuine assets to a minister of education. The most important trait is being a person of prayer and a student of the Bible. Everything we do should be prefaced with prayer. As we study God's Word, we mature as Christians. Having prayed about the direction of the educational program, we can face with confidence the task that is ours. One who knows the Bible is better equipped to lead others to be Bible teachers.

The minister of education needs to be a good organizer. She needs to recognize the value of planning. Administrative tasks require skill in organizing. Good organization produces quality meetings. Time is a precious commodity. People expect to receive something worthwhile from the time they give.

Good organization enables people to share responsibility. The more people involved in the life of the church the better. When people accept a responsibility, they need a job description. Often we become disgruntled with a person's performance when they received poor enlistment or training for the job.

Good communication skills are an asset to the minister of education. Involving the proper people in the decision-making process prepares the way for smoother changes. Keeping communication lines open prevents many problems. Being a good communicator to the church at large is important. Through announcements in church services, bulletins, and newspaper articles, church members become informed. Communicating effectively through the written and spoken word is valuable to the minister of education.

One of the most visible skills of a minister of education is being a good teacher. I like to think of the minister of education as being an equipper of the saints (see Eph. 4:12). Numerous opportunities present themselves for the minister of education to be a teacher of teachers. Teaching provides an excellent opportunity to model good teaching methods.

A pastor's wife who loves and cooperates with people possesses qualities vital to effective ministry. When people sense that you care about them, they have a greater desire to cooperate. Genuine expressions of appreciation to those with whom we work can make a difference in our ministry. Peter reminded us that "love covers a multitude of sins" (1 Pet. 4:8, RSV). When we are loving, caring leaders, people will be more tolerant of our own shortcomings.

An indispensable trait of the minister of education is being an avid reader. The informed pastor's wife is a definite asset to the church and her educational program. One church member, referring to his pastor's wife, said: "She usually knows what you ask her. If she doesn't know, she knows where to find the answer." That knowledge comes from extensive reading. What to read will be dealt with later.

Southern Baptists provide many excellent opportunities for training in the field of religious education. The pastor's wife who receives a seminary education is professionally trained to be a minister of education. Student wives, attending evening classes, may receive leadership training.

Every pastor's wife will not be able to avail herself of seminary training. Other avenues for preparation to serve as minister of education exist. One of these is through the Seminary Extension Department of the Southern Baptist Convention, located in Nashville, Tennessee. This study may be provided through a Seminary Extension center or through home study. There are courses in the biblical, theological-historical, and practical areas.

A second opportunity for leadership preparation is through state and local conferences. Regional conferences designed for associational ASSIST team leaders are excellent means of learning how to teach various ages. If one cannot attend these, associational workshops and clinics are available. These conference leaders have been trained by state leaders in their field of expertise and can train others.

The third opportunity for leadership training is at Ridgecrest and Glorieta Baptist Conference Centers. These centers provide the best opportunity for seeing firsthand how to teach various ages. Conferences for ministers of education are held which cover the various aspects of this ministry. A goal of any church leader should be to attend Glorieta or Ridgecrest. The pastor's wife will benefit by availing herself of this opportunity.

A fourth opportunity is provided by the Church Program Training Center at the Baptist Sunday School Board. Schedules of conferences are sent to churches each year. A wide range of subjects is covered for the professionally trained and the volunteer.

State and national Southern Baptist leaders will assist the local church in evaluating its educational program. Baptist Sunday School Board consultants as well as state leaders can give the pastor's wife assistance.

In addition to the above resources, there are printed materials to keep the minister of education informed. The *Mailbag,* which comes with each quarterly literature order form, has information on new resources. *Facts and Trends* is a news and information publication sent each month to staff members. *The Baptist Program* is another monthly periodical that keeps readers informed about Southern Baptist life.

There are several excellent books for the minister of education. *The Minister of Education as Educator, The Work of the Minister of Education, The Minister of Education as a Growth Agent,* and *The Ministry of Religious Education* (BBS) are some which are available. The Church Administration Department of the Baptist Sunday School Board semiannually produces a complimentary cassette tape which is sent to ministers of education. This tape provides up-to-date information on areas of concern and interest to ministers of education. Videotapes are becoming more popular as a means of training for various leadership positions. These tapes may be obtained from the nearest Baptist Film Center. Churches with the proper equipment will profit from BTN's training programs.

The leadership periodicals published by the various Convention agencies give outstanding help in directing the educational program. Being an avid reader facilitates the work of the minister of education. There are many publications which come across your desk which can give direction to your work.

Numerous sources of literature are on the market today. Southern Baptists have some of the least expensive and best literature available. Our literature is doctrinally sound with a balanced treatment of varying interpretations of Scripture.

Southern Baptist literature is also developmentally sound. The ages and stages of individuals are considered in preparing the literature. Those who write know the interests, abilities, and needs of the ages for whom they write.

Choices of literature have increased, with literature now being designed for both small and large churches. Literature is available for the mentally retarded, the blind, the deaf, and for those with limited reading ability. The _Church Materials Catalog_ provides information on all types of literature.

Some of the best products in recent years are the Equipping Center modules. These modules provide training and learning on a wide range of subjects. Church Training is an excellent time to use these modules. For those without a Church Training program, Equipping Centers could stimulate a renewed interest in training. Our own Church Training attendance increases when we offer Equipping Centers. Many, who will not attend an ongoing Church Training group, participate in training through Equipping Centers.

The Church Study Course system affords an excellent opportunity for in-service training. The minister of education, as well as church members, will grow through these studies. Using these courses for leadership training will improve the quality of education in the local church.

Relationship to Pastor-husband
The pastor's wife who assumes the position of minister of education encounters a new relationship with her husband. Their

relationship becomes one of a supervisor and an employee. The pastor's wife must realize emotionally as well as intellectually that he is the pastor and she is responsible to him for what she does. The pastor's wife should not assume too much authority or give the appearance of trying to run things. She should never undermine his leadership but give him her genuine support. A team spirit enhances the work of the pastor and his wife.

Good communication may prevent problems from arising in this unique relationship. The pastor should be informed of plans and goals of the minister of education. Scheduled staff meetings may be the means of informing the pastor. A "meeting of the minds" is needed on the pacing of progress. When one staff member moves faster than the other, some agreement on timing must be reached. A ministerial couple at odds is more detrimental to the church than two staff members who are not married.

Husbands and wives will not always agree on a certain course of action. As each gives and takes, they can come to agreement. The ability to see differences as staff related, not spouse related, can prevent conflict in the marriage. Differences of opinion will occur regardless of the work situation.

Clear guidelines of responsibility need to be worked out between the pastor and his wife. These guidelines can prevent friction from arising over the wife's assuming too much responsibility. Some pastors may need to be informed of the various aspects of religious education.

The biggest problem for pastors and wives working together seems to be limiting talk about church. One pastor's wife said: "When I have a new project, I am excited and want to talk about it too much. I have to make myself hush." She is not alone in her dilemma. Traveling back and forth to church invites constant "church talk." The pastor and his wife need to agree on time off from church.

Time alone away from the pressures of ministry deserves our attention. My husband and I reserve one day a week in which we usually leave town for the day. Those days are special and give us a new outlook when we return home. Because of encroaching responsibilities, we do not always get those days off; but it is our goal. Time together is something all couples need to strive for and make happen. To spend time together away from everyday responsibilities requires planning and commitment to each other.

Balancing time with your spouse and your children is quite a feat. Children have a way of demanding your attention. Pastors generally take time off to be with their families. Usually the children are the ones to reap the benefits of this time. Quality time alone as husband and wife is difficult to seize. In homes where mother and father are both church employees, some precautions are necessary. We want to avoid the children's becoming bitter because of the time the church demands of their parents. "Roast church" for dinner should not be served to children. Communicating proper motives for service will help instill positive attitudes toward church.

A ministering couple needs time apart as well as time together. Serving together can require too much togetherness. Each spouse needs to develop individual interests. Those interests might include clubs, sports, arts and crafts, music, or drama.

True joy in service can come to the couple who works at healthy professional and family relationships. Respect for each other's strengths and weaknesses enhances the relationship. A spirit of mutual love, understanding, cooperation, and communication fosters a sound relationship.

Relationship to the Church

The pastor's wife who serves as minister of education has a unique relationship with the congregation. She is first of all the pastor's wife. Everything she does is colored by the fact that she is his wife. Many church members will relate to her solely as pastor's wife. Church leaders will relate to her as minister of education when she is working with them in that capacity. She is more visible than the pastor's wife who takes the role of background supporter. Some church members may view her as the assistant pastor. Dispelling this notion and replacing it with a legitimate concept of the educational ministry takes time and conscious effort.

Demonstrating warmth, concern, love, and friendliness creates good rapport with the congregation. When we arrived at our present pastorate, I began sitting with different members of the congregation each service. Age made no difference. Making conversation with those I sat by at the close of the service helped us to get to know one another. I feel loved and accepted, and they convey to me that they feel the same way.

It is vital that the pastor's wife work within the existing church structures to accomplish her goals. Working through cliques in the church is deadly. Respect for church organization lends credibility to one's work. The organization may need changing, but doing so through appropriate channels is necessary.

The pastor's wife serving as minister of education should serve on the Church Council. She should also serve on the Sunday School and Church Training councils if they exist. Her role is to lend guidance in the planning and promotion of church goals and programs. These councils plan a calendar of events and coordinate the various organizations of the church.

By virtue of her position, the minister of education may serve on various committees. If she is not a member of the committee, she may be requested to contribute input into the committee's work. The pastor's wife may be asked to serve on the nominating committee. She can provide valuable input as to the most capable leaders. She must not be seen as pushing the pastor's choice for the position. Hopefully she will convey authentic concern for the best leaders for the congregation.

She will most likely be asked to make some budget recommendations. Requests for Vacation Bible School, literature, furnishings, and equipment may be her responsibility. The Sunday School and Church Training directors may seek her assistance in determining their budget requests.

The minister of education has a unique relationship with

the organizations of the church. The most important of these relationships is with the Sunday School. The Sunday School is the barometer of the life of the church. A strong Sunday School produces church growth both numerically and spiritually.

The minister of education should lead in enlisting and training the teachers and officers of the Sunday School. Southern Baptists have some excellent resources to aid in these responsibilities: *How to Discover, Enlist, and Train Sunday School Workers; How to Start and Maintain a Weekly Workers' Meeting; How to Improve Bible Teaching and Learning in the Sunday School: Pastor-Director Guide;* and *Training Potential Sunday School Workers* (BBS). Organizing an ongoing training program is an important task of the minister of education.

The minister of education should plan regularly with the Sunday School director as well as the total Sunday School leadership. Keeping these leaders informed of current information is important. Much information will cross your desk. Everything cannot be promoted. Knowing your congregation and what its needs are determines the emphases.

Outreach deserves the attention and leadership of the minister of education. A regular visitation program is vital to the life of the church. Church members need to be trained in evangelistic visitation. Two resources of help in this area are *How to Set Up and Conduct a Weekly Visitation Program* and *Training Outreach Workers for the Sunday School* (BBS).

The Sunday School merits a large percentage of your time because of its significance to the church. People need to know God's Word. They deserve well-trained, dedicated teachers.

The minister of education also works closely with the Church Training organization. Trained church members make better leaders. New church members and new Christians need to be trained. Church Training provides an opportunity for this training. Church Training can take place at times and places other than the traditional ones. Conferences, retreats, and seminars are other approaches to training church members to become leaders.

The WMU and Brotherhood need the support and guidance of the minister of education. The pastor's wife may have a greater influence and better rapport than even the pastor, especially with the WMU. In the age of Bold Mission Thrust, an informed and enthusiastic pastor's wife can contribute much to the church's awareness of mission needs.

Genuine appreciation expressed regularly to lay leaders gives added incentive to do their best. Love and confidence in those with whom we serve produces a spirit of cooperation and harmony.

Benefits of Service
Many churches depend on their pastor for leadership in the area of education, but the pastor may consider the educational program at the bottom of his priority list. In a survey conducted by the Sunday School Board, education and counseling were ranked last in a list of priorities.[3] Churches where the pastor serves as his own minister of education may need additional help. The pastor's wife often has the qualifications to do the job. She is already on the field. She cares about her husband's ministry. A pastor can give quality leadership to just so many areas. The common goals of a pastor and his wife can heighten their ministry to the church. The results will be better teachers, better resources, and better coordination and promotion of the church's programs.

The pastor also benefits when his wife serves as minister of education. He is working with someone whose approach he knows well. He has already developed a working relationship through marriage. The two can give team leadership.

The pastor's wife serving as minister of education frees the pastor from much administrative detail. The survey mentioned earlier indicated that church administration was just above education and counseling in priority.[4] Pastors with a strong sense of calling to proclamation are often not inclined toward the details of administration. The pastor's wife can be an asset to her husband in areas of administration, and she can keep abreast of resources that her husband does not have time to read.

The pastor's wife can handle situations which do not require the pastor's attention. On many occasions I am consulted about educational matters. The pastor has enough responsibility without having to deal with situations which can be handled by someone else. The pastor is then free to use his time on areas of higher priority or more pressing need.

Few wives can become so intimately involved in their husband's job. The pastor's wife has that opportunity. She can experience great satisfaction in being an integral part of her husband's ministry.

Seeing the spiritual growth and leadership development of church members is one of the greatest joys of service. Suzanne was shy, lacking in self-confidence. With encouragement, training, and her personal determination to serve God, she has become an excellent adult teacher. Wanda loves preschoolers. She has taken advantage of training opportunities at church, in the association, and regional conferences. Today she is preschool coordinator. Preschoolers receive quality teaching at church because of her work with other teachers. Hearing words of gratitude for the confidence expressed toward lay leaders is another joy of service.

The pastor's wife benefits from serving as minister of education. This staff position gives the pastor's wife the opportunity to use her God-given talents. Many pastors' wives have the abilities needed to serve as minister of education. Feeling God's call and having the opportunity to serve produce deep satisfaction.

Serving a God who loved us enough to give his Son brings unsurpassed joy.

----

[1]Dianne Cooksey Kessler, "Old Roles and New Symbols: Female Administrators in Transition," *The Christian Century* (November 11, 1981), p. 1163.
[2]Ibid.

[3]J. Clifford Tharp, Jr., "The Pastor Serving as His Own Minister of Education," Research Services Department, Sunday School Board of the Southern Baptist Convention, May 1983, p. 16.
[4]Ibid.

"The singing is mighty good this morning," Phil Parttime affirmed. "Now before we take up the offering, everybody turn to number 437; and let's all sing the first, second, and last verses."

Brother Loner cringed. It was no wonder the church was having a hard time paying its bills. Why did Phil pick "In the Sweet By and By" for an offertory hymn about three times out of every four? Loner had been planning to talk to Phil about this problem for months, but there never seemed to be time for them to get together for planning. Phil drove a truck for a bakery in one of the larger towns nearby. He was usually available only minutes before time for the worship services to begin.

Well, at least Loner hoped that the special music wouldn't be something like "Precious Memories." Nothing could be worse than that; at least he thought so.

When the offering was concluded, Phil went back to the pulpit, not to sing himself but to introduce a "guest soloist." The guest, it turned out, was the woman who had been rather conspicuously seated on the first row on the left side. Both her dress and her quasi-religious song would have been more apt for the Rainbow Room down the street.

Phil was as good as gold but as green as a gourd. Brother Loner loved him like a son but was often thrown into near panic by some of the things he did. There was no doubt about it, they were just going to have to find some time for planning.

—George Clark

Chapter 7

Pastor and Part-time Minister of Education Working Together

David W. Hayes

The chapters preceding this one have given you good information and advice concerning you, as pastor, meeting the needs of your congregation in the area of Christian education. There is a point, however, past which your leadership will start losing its force. Because of the sheer size and scope of your ministry, you will need to get help from someone trained and experienced in church programs. You probably already have a part-time staff member leading your church's music program. Most pastors never consider leading their own music program. Why not get help with your educational program as well?

Here are some signs that it's time to turn your educational duties over to someone else:

1. People begin asking you about literature you've never heard of—a sign that you can't keep up with new products.

2. People begin asking you about approaches to teaching you've never heard of—a sign that you can't keep up with all new programs.

3. People begin asking you for help, and you can't remember which job they have accepted—a sign that you can't keep up with your program structure.

4. People begin asking you for the same help over and over—a sign that you're trying to do too much by yourself.

If, after examining your ministry and seeking wisdom through prayer, you feel led to ask your congregation to call a part-time minister of education, there are some things you need to decide *before* going to the church.

Getting Started

What does the church want?—Any problems encountered in the four areas listed above should give you a strong clue to the direction the church wants to go. The solution to most problems in the education ministry of the church is organization which, in turn, flows from a combination of knowledge and experience. Look at the programs of your church as they are now: Sunday School, Church Training, missions education. Where do you need strength for growth? Where is leadership from within the church already strong enough? The part-time staffer you will seek probably won't be equally knowledgeable in all three of these program areas. Decide in which area(s) the church wants or needs growth.

What is part-time?—A part-time staff position has been described as part-time pay for a full-time job. That is why professionals use the term *bivocational*. The description of what you expect from a part-time staffer is a combination of how much time you expect to be spent and what the result must be. Here are some steps or stages of time involvement:

- Be present for Sunday programs and worship
- Be present for Wednesday programs
- Be involved in visitation
- Be involved in church staff planning meetings
- Be involved in church program planning meetings
- Accompany church members on retreats, etc.
- Attend associational meetings

Here are some levels or stages of the scope of responsibility the person will have; that is, expected results:

- Sunday School and Church Training
- Visitation program
- Missions education programs
- A youth ministry beyond educational programs
- Special studies such as January Bible Study
- Special emphases such as Life Commitment Sunday

- Vacation Bible School
- Planning and leading in church retreats

Studying these two lists will help you realize two things: First, your part-time minister of education can only be there for so many hours; and second, your part-time minister of education is capable of doing only so much. Any person will have limits. How much one person can get done in a definite amount of time will be a combination of knowledge and experience plus the working environment of your church. The knowledge and experience needed to accomplish the assigned responsibilities in the time expected to be given to the job will give you some indication of the salary you will want to offer.

What salary should the church offer?—The salary you attach to the position is a measure of how important the position is to your church. You are deciding to employ someone because the person has special knowledge and experience. Later in this chapter you will find suggestions for other ways of compensation if the salary is necessarily low. Guidance on specific salary levels can be obtained from your association or state convention offices.

What does the church want? What is part-time? What salary should the church offer? The church is looking to you for guidance in these areas. Once you have decided what you need, you are ready to start looking.

Looking for Talent

Before you get too far in your search, let's consider some alternatives. There are ways of borrowing talent without having to add another employee to your staff. They include:

Soliciting help from the association or state convention office.—Sometimes these people will work with a church for a quarter or longer to help develop your existing programs and add new ones. They may even suggest people for your part-time staff position when you choose to add one.

Consulting with a minister of education from another church.—Although you can't expect a lot of time, what this person can do can make a difference through such avenues as quarterly teachers' meetings or consultation on specific problems. This type of help may be available from denominations other than Southern Baptist, particularly in areas where our denomination is in the pioneer stages of its work.

Sharing a staff member with another church.—There is a lot of precedent for this in our history. Churches used preachers either riding a circuit or serving two or more churches near each other. You can share the salary expense and use the staffer's services to the extent of your contribution. One way to test the water for this alternative is to hold a joint Vacation Bible School with another church with a consolidated faculty from both congregations. You may begin to check on this or other suggestions at pastors' conferences or other meetings.

Getting help from a Christian college or seminary.—These schools have lots of young Christian men and women who have gained some knowledge and want to use it in a practical way. You can get several helpers for the salary expense of one part-time professional.

Calling a Part-time Minister of Education

But if you feel you need someone dedicated to your church's needs, then get your own part-time minister of education. Once you know what you want and the range of your expectations, develop a job description. List responsibilities and discuss that list with prospective staffers. Form a personnel committee, if you don't have one already; and work with them in recruiting. This step will bring church members into the decision-making process and help you ensure that the needs, wants, and desires of the members are being met along with the goals you feel led to pursue.

Have your personnel committee interview prospective staff members. Let them do the talking so you won't appear to be railroading the decision process. Then, when the committee selects someone, they should bring the motion to the church. Bring the motion on Sunday when the most members will be present. Let the church see and meet your prospect. Be sure

the motion includes the job description and salary. Announce
your intention to call someone in advance to allow for maximum involvement. The initial success of your new part-time
minister of education will depend on having the church members involved in the decision to call a new staff member.

And when you have called your part-time staffer, pause,
thank God, ask for help, and then go for it!

Beginning a New Relationship
You are the pastor of a church. You have been called by the
church, led by the Holy Spirit, to be responsible for the spiritual welfare of this congregation. With the addition of another staff member, you are now the head of the church staff.
Some good guidance on this role may be obtained from the
publications of the Sunday School Board, most notably
Church Administration magazine (MS) and *Church Staff
Teams That Win* by Jerry Brown (BBS).

Your work with a part-time staff in the area of education
begins with a time for growth. It is so important during this
period to keep the lines of communication open between the
two of you. Because no two persons will have the same talents, your part-time minister of education will have strengths
and weaknesses which you will need to consider. Allow your
M.E. to begin slowly and move at his/her own speed. Allow
room for growth and exploration, to learn and to experiment.
Don't bill your M.E. as an expert or as someone who will solve
all your problems. Don't dump all your educational duties at
once; allow time for transition.

Duties were listed and a job description was developed before the M.E. was hired. Use these as a benchmark for your
discussions together. Share your sense of priorities within the
list of duties. What is more critical now, as you begin your
work together, visitation or planning, missions education or
Church Training? Lead your church through the transition
time on a deliberate course. Be supportive of your minister of
education. Don't continue your old educational tasks and thus
make your staffer a second-class leader. Here are some spe-

cific points:

Your M.E. should expect you to:
• show enthusiastic support.
• display authority and competence in your role as pastor and head of the staff.
• be present at special events.
• keep other programs, such as the music ministry, from competing with the education ministry (and vice versa).
• emphasize the educational ministry occasionally in sermons, announcements, and conversation.
• be a pastor to the M.E. and his family.
• support the M.E. and the educational ministry in prayer.
Your M.E. may ask you to:
• join in teachers' meetings and other nonstaff planning.
• involve yourself in settling disputes or counseling.
• lead in studying a special emphasis.
Your M.E. should forget (unless you tell him otherwise):
• expecting you to fill in as a substitute teacher.
• expecting you to prepare a lesson or join a class.
• expecting you to be an expert on education.

Something magical happens when people called together by God begin on a course of action in his will. If you are led by the same Spirit, you will be led in the same direction. To keep the magic alive will take a joint effort on your part. You will need to go through a period of original planning and a time of sensitizing to help you work together.

Planning with Your Part-time Minister of Education
There is a point in this beginning process when everyone must sit down and put the program on paper. This is the first crucial test of your ability to lead your education program through others. It is the written contract between your minister of education, volunteer education leaders, and the church. It is planning, and nothing is more difficult or more important.

For you as the pastor it will be difficult. As mentioned earlier, you probably have a part-time music leader already. But a pastor doesn't mind turning music responsibilities over to others. Indeed, it's something that is axiomatic—expected by the church and by its preacher. It isn't as easy with the educational programs. You are probably more familiar with Sunday School and RAs. You have no doubt been involved with your missions leaders during times of special emphases. Chances are you even meet with your Sunday School director regularly. Your person and personality are ingrained in your church's fabric. How you go about turning these areas of involvement over to another is critical to the success of your new staffer.

Make no mistake about it. You must turn them over. If you do not, then your minister of education becomes ineffective and will either sit down to do nothing or rise up to leave. If you are a parent, you can imagine the problems that would arise if your child bypassed you to get permission. Your line of authority must be clearly defined and always followed. You are head of the staff, not the entire staff.

Setting priorities.—Talk to your minister of education about his abilities and the church's expectations. In order to maximize his effectiveness, you may have to decide to approach the church's priorities in a different order or in different strengths. No person is a perfect fit with any job description. The M.E. must likewise be sensitive to the church's desires and make them priorities. You need to help align the person and the task.

Let's approach this systematically. Sit down with the list you and the personnel committee developed originally. Then rewrite the list based on your discussions with your new minister of education. Notice two things. First, what has disappeared from the first list or appeared new on the second? Second, what is on the second list but was reprioritized? This is your first hurdle because something someone thought important isn't where they saw it last.

If, for example, a group of parents has pressed for recreation for their kids and your new staffer is not adept at this or hasn't the time for such extensive nonchurch hours, you need to tell them that this area of ministry will have to be supported by volunteer leaders within the church. Ask for their help.

Include someone from each group in the planning process. It's your responsibility as pastor to bring the needs, wants, and desires of the congregation in line with the reality of the situation. Don't saddle your part-timer with that at the beginning. You know the church members; the new M.E. doesn't. You can gradually share information with the M.E. about the church's formal and informal power structures.

Planning activities.—Establishing the planning group comes next. Let me suggest a Church Council as a good planning nucleus. Many churches already have one. More than anything else, the Church Council will approve your planning and legitimize the role of your M.E.

Using this body composed of leaders from each program area plus staff helps you in three ways:

1. No area is left out.

2. Friction between programs is reduced by ensuring that conflicting schedules will not arise.

3. Program inflation is reduced. This occurs when special emphasis is shown in one ministry area such as education.

Plan your meeting. As pastor, you are head of the Church Council. Good plans are the result of good meetings, and good meetings are the result of good planning. Sit down with your lists and your desires and talk to the Lord about them.

Pick your meeting time and place, and set the agenda. These are all duties of the senior person and are important. Your meeting needs to be held when the majority can attend, but you'll never meet everyone's needs. The smaller church can often do best on Sunday afternoon before the evening program begins. Allow an hour. Less time may keep you from completing plans for an important emphasis. Too much time may allow too much unnecessary debate.

By the end of the meeting you should have done the following: (1) affirmed the priorities you have set, (2) defined dates for key events, (3) defined responsibilities for events, and (4) set the next meeting. It is a great feeling to have this firmly in place.

Avoiding Problems

One final word of warning to you in getting started with your new minister of education. It has been said that anyone among strangers becomes a consultant. Because your M.E. part-time staffer has specialized education, training, or experience, he or she may approach the job as if to give advice. Planning your meeting and observing your M.E. during this first get-together will give you a clue to whether you have a worker or a sitter. Here are some signs you may have a problem:

• If he takes an "us" and "them" approach and sounds like an elitist, he will not work well in a small church. Smaller churches often think of their staff members as invited guests and don't want someone who stays outside the group.

• If she fails to show respect for you as pastor and leader of the staff, you could have two problems. First, she must recognize her programs as subordinate to the total ministry of the church of which you are head. Second, the church respects you as its leader and will not like anyone's not showing you respect.

• If he instructs people instead of leading them, he will not earn their respect. Church members want to think of their leaders as part of the workers in the church. Never lose sight of the fact that it is always the church members who collectivly do most of the work.

Worried? Don't be. If you have reservations, now is the time to clear them up. Talk to your staffer about the need to be directly involved in the work of the church, that she needs to respect you as leader and that she, in turn, must lead others. This will get you back on the right foot. But, if she cannot reconcile herself to this, let her go before she starts. The apostle Paul traveled a long time with Demas only to lose his co-worker (see Tim. 4:10). It is possible for it to happen to you.

But if you get off to a good start, praise God!

Developing an Ongoing Relationship
Praise God indeed! Good programs don't just happen; they
are caused. God has set the example by planning for our salvation, for the role of his church over the millennia. What is an
hour of our time? Your first Church Council meeting behind
you and your relationship with your staffer secure, let us begin.

Don't forget your music or other staff and don't forget those
laypersons who did the work before you got your M.E. Your
minister of music didn't replace the choir members or the
pianist. Your minister of education should not replace a Sunday School director. The idea is to aid good people to serve
better.

The primary task of a staff member is to help others serve.—
Strengthen existing programs, but strive for newness—not at
the expense of your ongoing church ministries but to reinforce the basic desires of those programs. For an example, the
DiscipleYouth approach to Church Training does not replace
Youth Church Training but reinforces its basic purpose, to
motivate and equip young people for Christ. The WIN program does not eliminate visitation but is merely a different
approach to reaching others for Christ.

Allow your new M.E. to start from scratch, even to have a
year of jubilee and let a program rest. No one can cover all the
bases at first. The Lord calls those with talents for the immediate task and abilities to be developed for future tasks. Starting with the priorities you established with your M.E. and
sticking to them will be of great benefit. Birth is easier than
resurrection, but with God all things are possible. Just take
your time.

At this point in your work together, you will leave the for-
mality of writing job descriptions and establishing priorities
and begin to establish your working relationship. The hard
work you did in determining the kind of person your church
needs, the preparations you made in bringing the church and
your new M.E. together, and your dedication in leading your
congregation to this point are now ready to bear fruit.

Building bridges of understanding is really easy, but you have to want to build them. Developing good staff relationships is a lot like building a successful marriage, something that takes effort but is worth it. Watching others grow as you stand still is no fun. Actually, this is an excellent opportunity for growth in your life both spiritually and professionally. Begin by being overwhelmed at the opportunities before you. That will bring you closer to God through prayer and the daily walk you will continue to have with him.

Look at yourself and the prejudices you are bringing into the relationship. You could have formed a negative opinion from a former M.E. or one at a church you pastored earlier in your life. Events at other churches in your area or even something that happened while you were a young man can become a blockage to your relationship. If your M.E. is a woman, you may need to reevaluate your opinions of women in ministry. If you are a pastor who hasn't always understood the actions of your music leader or become dismayed at the way some people carry out their ministry, you should make every effort to clear away any doubts you may have.

Take the list you drew up earlier of things your new M.E. is expected to accomplish. Then make your own list of things you want to accomplish, starting with things you have wanted to do for some time. Now add it to new things you feel able to strive for since you have an additional part-time staffer. These may include more visitation, an opportunity for more personal Bible study, more education, and an all-important priority—more time with your family.

Typically, a pastor who has led his church through a time of growth has overextended himself. One of the hardest things, as we already discussed, will be stepping back from being still involved in everything. Being able to share with your congregation the blessings you have received from studying the Word and spending time with your family will also aid you in avoiding a problem some staff members experience when duties are handed down channel to another person—the notion that a leader is doing less for the church. Keeping lines of communication open with the formal and informal leadership will always be important. You will sometimes have to handle a problem brought to you instead of your M.E. because you are the pastor. The ultimate responsibility is still yours.

Your list of new things to accomplish should excite and challenge you and lead you to prayer. It is a great thing to see God's plan unfold before you! Next, grow in closeness to your congregation. Another problem which often develops during growth is that a pastor becomes channeled into dealing with a few people and misses the ninety and nine. Since you will have to spend less time on educational responsibilities, you can spend more time with more of your people.

Your part-time M.E. should free you to grow. Your leadership should aid him in growth. You must support your part-timer from a distance, up close, directly, and behind the scenes. Show your support by making rounds with him occasionally during Sunday School. Be seen together by the church. Let him make announcements during worship or lead prayer meeting in your absence. A little "proud father" is especially helpful to a young person and places your role in the correct context for your congregation.

Remember, there's no limit to what can be accomplished if you don't care who gets the credit. The best approach is to give God the glory. That will link you, all your staff, and congregation together solidly.

Continuing Success

After your initial success and the blessings the Lord has bestowed on you are bearing fruit, you must develop a plan for continuing success. Much like the conquering army needs to know what it will do after the battle, you must have a plan to handle your success.

Delegation without design is abdication. At this point take another hard look at your program component and ask yourself these questions:

Have we followed the priorities set forth by the church?—If not, are the differences the result of changes within the church's needs or the result of personal preferences by you, your minister of education, or certain church members? It is important to evaluate periodically your course.

Are the program components operating efficiently?—If not, have you stayed too long with programs that are not responsive or perhaps brought in something new and not in keeping with your church's personality? It is important to have your Church Council keep tabs on the programs represented by its membership and to make sure everything is operating smoothly. If not, then your M.E. needs to implement change.

Are the elected program leaders carrying out their responsibilities?—If not, is training needed or has the church put itself in a rut by reelecting people who can't administer changed programs? This may well be your toughest evaluation and one best discussed in nominating committee. This is also a problem area you may have to handle yourself because your part-time staffer may not yet understand the interpersonal relationships of the church as well as you do.

An excellent method of planning for success is for your M.E. to turn program components over to lay members for leadership. This is done on a gradual basis over time to allow her to assist laypersons in getting started. She can then devote her time elsewhere, and your church gets more involved in its own ministry.

Perhaps your next step is going from a part-time to a full-time M.E. The next chapter in this book speaks to that. One thing is sure; the best foundation for a full-timer is a good experience with a part-timer.

Your decision to call a part-time M.E. is the beginning of a great opportunity for you and your church. Carefully planned and carried out, it can be the best years in your total experience with your church, an opportunity to bring someone into your fold, to grow together in the Lord, and then, when the fullness of time is come, to move on to even higher ground. It is my prayer that you are given the opportunity to grow in God's grace through this co-ministry.

A soft moan escaped Brother Loner's lips as he slumped in the big chair behind his cluttered desk. He was tired—not merely fatigued but just plain tuckered out. There always seemed to be more work than there was week.

He had spent most of the evening at the hospital with Percy Puney. Today was Friday, and as yet he had no "word from the Lord." At times like this, he was sometimes tempted to wish that Baptist preachers really did get their sermons from Nashville.

Then there was that bunch of letters to committee chairmen to be written. Mary Jane Willing had been coming for a half day three days a week to do some secretarial work, but that barely gave her time to type the bulletin and keep the records up-to-date.

Frank Fumbler, the Sunday School director, did the best he could to keep his organizations oiled and running; but there was so much more that needed to be done.

The tithes and offerings had been improving at least a little bit over the past several months. And the building would be paid for in a little while. Wouldn't it be great, Loner thought, if maybe, just maybe, he could lead the church into calling another staff person? There'd have to be a really good job description. The people would need to have a clear understanding with the prospective staff member. But, if all of the pieces were put together correctly, it would be great!

As Brother Loner thought about what the addition of a fellow worker could mean, a peace settled over the study. Things became quite and still. The tired pastor had fallen asleep.

—George Clark

Chapter 8

When to Add a Staff Member

John R. Chandler

In the church where the pastor is the only staff member, he will do many tasks in addition to his pastoral duties. He may serve at various times as the Sunday School director, Church Training director, or song leader. He probably functions part of the time as custodian, printer, typist, or record keeper. Often, his wife will help with visitations, enlistment, and clerical duties.

When the church begins to grow, the pastor finds his work load increasing. He reaches a point when he cannot do all that must be done and still lead the church, nurture it into health, minister to persons in need, and preach effectively three times each week. He is busy but is not accomplishing primary tasks. He becomes frustrated and burned-out trying to do it all by himself.

A church must be alert to this situation, because the people need a pastor who can concentrate on being the pastor. The church needs a pastor who can devote his time to leading the church, caring for the members, and preaching the gospel. So, it becomes the responsibility of the church to add needed staff leaders at the appropriate time. If that step is delayed until a crisis occurs, it is detrimental to the church and the pastor.

A good staff development plan can be set up in four phases:
1. Add part-time custodial and secretarial work.
2. Move one or both part-time positions to full-time.

3. Add part-time staff for education, youth, or music to provide program leadership.
4. Add a full-time staff member in a position most needed.

Understanding the Requirements for Adding a Staff Member

Adding a staff member is an important step for both the church and the person who is called. Adding a new staff member is an act of faith. That step should grow out of deliberate prayer and study. Above all, it should be based on a clear and accurate understanding of the need, the congregation's expectations, and the potential congregational support.

Need
We can look at the possibility of adding a staff member when the time required for administrating and developing programs of education, ministry, and witnessing require another full-time leader.

If specific church programs require a full-time leader, options include minister of education, associate pastor, minister of music, or minister of youth. Frequently, the first full-time staff member is a combination assignment. The most common are minister of education and music, minister of education and youth, and minister of music and youth.

Expectations
Congregational awareness of staff roles, tasks, and the relationship between congregation and staff member sets the stage for an effective ministry. Expectations and awareness color attitudes toward a new staff member and, incidentally, toward those who make recommendations to the church. Expectations will give the new staff member permission to do the work and will provide support for the work when the load becomes difficult. Lack of support will show up when the new staff person tries to enlist leaders, schedule meetings, plan projects, use facilities, or obtain budget. Expectations be-

come the goals members have for this new work and form the basis of their evaluation of that work.

Forced termination of pastors and staff members has become a major concern among Southern Baptists in the eighties. Recent studies indicate that one of the reasons for forced termination is that a substantial conflict existed in the congregation before the minister was called. Unresolved conflict and alienated factions become the basis of future conflict between the minister and the congregation. Obviously, it is important to resolve conflict prior to calling a staff member. It is also important not to create conflict in the process of deciding to add a staff member.

Congregational Support

A new staff member can be added when the congregation can provide money for personnel and program costs, office space, and administrative equipment. Salary is the obvious cost you will consider. Likewise, you must consider the cost of providing an office, desk, chair, bookcase, file cabinet, and other equipment. Then the costs of operating an expanded educational program must be considered. Costs for leader training, promotion projects, brochures, stationery, postage, office supplies, and paper should be considered. One caution, don't build the expectation that the new staff member will pay for him/herself.

To add a new staff member the congregation must be willing to support the work. Consideration must be given to organization, schedules, enlistment procedures, and program coordination through which a new staff member must work.

People, time, money, facilities, and equipment are the resources that enable any effort to suceed. The willingness of the church to provide these resources is an indication that the church will support staff expansion. If the church will establish and follow good leader enlistment processes, if the church will establish and honor weekly schedules, and if the church will provide basic requirements of facilities and equipment, then it is ready to add a staff member.

Exploring the Requirements for Adding a Staff Member

How do we determine the need for another staff member?
The pastor and personnel committee should take the initiative for a staff development study. The purpose of the study is to develop recommendations that can be acted on by the church. The pastor and personnel committee should involve appropriate groups like the deacons, Church Council, Sunday School council, Church Training council, music council, finance committee, and property committee to obtain a broad base of participation. This will call out the best insights of the people and establish support for the new work.

If the church does not have a personnel committee, establishing one would be wise. That committee becomes responsible for recommending personnel policies and procedures to the church. They represent the interest of the church in personnel matters. They also represent the interests of the staff in relation to the church.

The first question to answer is, Do we need another staff member? Answering this question satisfactorily is the first and most important step. The need should be clear both to those who make the study and to the congregation. Jerry Brown in *Church Staff Teams That Win* suggested several additional questions to consider:

• What kind of ministry tasks need to be performed by this person to help the pastor and church accomplish their ministry?

• What kind of personal qualities are needed?

• What kind of skills are required?

Your new staff position will require special administrative and ministry skills. The requirements will be different from those of the pastor. Ministers of education and combination ministers will need good conceptual skills to develop, adapt, and refine Sunday School, Church Training, and missions programs. A music leadership position requires good musical skills. All staff ministers need leadership, administrative, and relational skills. Expectations of finding persons who can do all things, solve all problems, and perform all tasks because they are assigned by the church creates a weak foundation.

The new staff member and pastor must understand and appreciate each other's unique roles. Although they have different roles, they can become a team by sharing the same objectives and goals. The pastor should be the staff leader with supervisory responsibility. In addition, the pastor must be able to share leadership responsibility and affirm the other person.

Recognize that persons with different personalities, interests, and work styles bring added strength to a staff team. In fact, the art of building an effective staff team is to call persons whose strengths compliment rather than duplicate the pastor's. Different gifts, points of view, and work styles provide a wider range of insights, actions, and evaluations needed for good decision making and complete church program operation.

There are no simple guidelines or pat formulas to use in determining the need. However, the following conditions will help establish whether your church needs an additional staff member.

Consider the pastor's work load.—The pastor is a preacher, administrator, teacher, counselor, evangelist, minister, and representative of the church in the community. His work is seldom finished. As mentioned earlier, the pastor is a key in leading the church to see clearly God's mission for the congregation. The scope of his work enlarges when the size of the congregation increases. More members produce greater demands for his time.

Most people are aware that work always expands to fill all available time. Many church members only see the pastor as the preacher (two or three thirty-minute sermons a week) or the minister (occasional hospital and death visits). They do not see the time spent in sermon preparation, meetings, and counseling. They do not see the strong need for the pastor to give attention and time to his own spiritual development and to his family. Some church members may not realize that the effective ministry of a staff member demands time for all these things. The personnel committee can reinforce this concept with information to the congregation and thereby promote a healthy, mature relationship between the staff and the congregation.

Some church members don't believe the pastor can ever be overloaded. Therefore, the pastor, and possibly the personnel committee, must establish a common understanding about the time needed by the pastor to accomplish his work.

The pastor should set priorities for the work he does. Identify work that needs to be done but cannot be done because of time limitations. Establish a good estimate of how much time that additional work will require. Then, in order to provide a foundation of ownership among the congregation, involve a number of people in the study such as the personnel committee, deacons, Sunday School director, Church Training director, and finance committee chairman. They will provide support for proposals presented to the church in business meetings.

Church members must see the need for an additional full-time leader before they will support that work. Also, they must have adequate time to develop an acceptance of the idea.

Consider church trends in membership, attendance, and budget.—A growth pattern of increasing church membership and Sunday School enrollment is one indication of a good condition for adding a second staff member. The trend should have a good possibility of continuing upward. The following factors should be considered together in your recommendation to the church. The percentages and numerical figures listed are simply clues. Use these figures in your study as a starting point for committee discussions. You should fill in the figures that say to your church, "At this level, we will begin our search for a second staff member."

1. Church membership of __*400*__ with annual growth rate of __*5*__ %.

2. Sunday School attendance *250 to 300* with growth possibilities.
3. Budget of *$200,000* with *40* % available for salaries and benefits.
4. Large group of senior adults, singles, youth, or special interest group requiring special attention.
5. Presence of a sizable group of persons with special skills that could be mobilized in a special ministry team.

There are two critical points in church and Sunday School membership and attendance levels. First, is there potential for real growth? Second, can the church support a second ministerial staff person without making the pastor and the new person vulnerable to weak economical conditions?

Budget considerations should provide salary and benefits for the professional staff and necessary clerical workers, and financial support for church programs.

Each church determines salaries paid to employees of that church. Salaries should be set by studying the local professional and labor salaries, not just by comparing salaries with other churches. Salaries should be comparable to those positions in the community requiring similar education and experience. Benefits ought to include a pension plan, Social Security, a medical plan, and life insurance. A benefits package should include vacation, holidays, sick leave with pay, paid expenses for educational meetings and personal development conferences, and professional time away. A benefits package also may include a Christmas gift, a housing allowance, a personal library allowance, and a parking space. The church may pay all or part of a particular benefit, or a staff member may contribute to a benefit to increase insurance or retirement coverage. A church can help establish stability in staff tenure by providing an adequate salary program.

Some churches treat car allowances and conference attendance as benefits. In reality, local transportation related to work and participation in leadership training conferences and conventions benefit the church; both are essential for staff persons to perform their responsibilities. These should be considered expenses and paid on a reimbursement basis.

Because a church is located near a pocket of special interest groups, adding a staff member to lead work addressing the needs of that group may be desirable. These might include senior adults, singles, youth, students, special education, and handicapped persons.

In a few situations, a church may find that they have a sizable group of persons with specialized skills that can be mobilized for ministry. This might be true if they are near a medical school, university, military base, or major industry. The specialized ministry could be the use of those skills in ministry or witness to the community. For example, the presence of a number of medical personnel might open the possibility for a ministry to underprivileged or economically deprived persons or senior adults. A second dimension might be to develop caring, sharing, and witnessing groups to minister to persons in the school, base, industry, or profession.

Consider community trends.—Population and building trends in your community will play a major role in the potential growth of your church. Look at the activity in your community in the following areas.

• Population shifts which increase the number of prospects.
• Construction of new homes or apartments.
• Growth of special needs groups in the community.

If growth potential exists, your church should seriously consider adding full-time staff.

How do we discover the expectations and awareness of the congregation?

The personnel committee and pastor need to be able to say to a candidate for a new staff position, "We represent our church." In order to represent the congregation faithfully, the committee needs specific information from the congregation. Three steps can provide that information.

1. The church in business meeting assigns study and plan-

ning responsibility to the personnel committee.

2. The committee discusses the need for an additional staff member with small groups such as Sunday School teachers and officers, Church Training groups, WMU groups, Brotherhood groups, Music Ministry groups, and deacons.

3. The committee conducts written response surveys in worship services.

Discussions and written responses should center on three questions: First, what is your thinking concerning the role of the pastor and a new staff member? Second, what do you expect a new staff member to do? Third, what will be his or her most important duty? second most important duty? third most important duty?

Be sure to have someone make notes during discussions with small groups. Read the recorded information back to the group to ensure the correctness of statements. In this way, both you and the participants will have a clear understanding of the information gathered through the discussions.

Determining What Action Our Church Should Take Before Looking for a New Staff Member

The first action is to decide to add a new staff by vote in a business meeting. Then, follow-up actions are needed to support that decision and lay the foundation for an effective ministry by that staff member.

1. Develop a search and calling plan.
2. Adopt job description and salary benefits plan.
3. Provide office space and equipment.
4. Budget personnel expenses.
5. Budget for expanded program expenses.

The personnel committee should develop a plan for finding and calling the staff member, and present that plan to the church for information. The plan will establish how the committee will operate clarifying who, what, and when (sequence) of each action. Clarify for the church how the committee plans to obtain names of candidates. The plan may establish a time and way for the committee to make progress reports. Follow-up actions 2 through 5 (listed above) will require church action on each.

Do's and Don'ts for Screening and Calling

Not all persons who are pressed into service on personnel committees are comfortable in screening, interviewing, and recommending candidates to the church. Others will have no problem with the assignment because they have similar responsibilities in their work. However, all should recognize the unique relationship they have with their church. It will be the church that calls the staff member, not the committee employing the staff member on behalf of the church.

Based on the experiences of other committees and churches, here are some things to do that will make your work more effective.

1. Develop and have an adopted job description to use in the screening and interviewing process.

2. Establish minimum educational, experience, and skill qualifications to use in considering candidates.

3. Contact the director of missions, state minister relations director, appropriate state convention program directors, selected pastors and church staff persons, and seminaries for recommendations. Seek recommendations from numerous sources. Don't rely on one person outside the committee, thus allowing that person to control the committee's decision.

4. Check out all recommendations thoroughly. Look at what is not being said as well as what is said.

5. Develop and have adopted a salary and benefits plan to share with candidates.

6. Plan interview questions in advance.

7. Make your plans clear to candidates you interview and reimburse expenses immediately.

Occasionally, problems develop in the interviewing and calling process that can be embarrassing to the church and to potential staff members. The don'ts listed are intended to help you avoid those situations.

1. Don't add a new staff member as a status symbol.

2. Don't ask the congregation for names. To do so tends to obligate the committee to "hear my man."

3. Don't invite friends or mates to travel with the committee to hear or interview a prospect. This in effect enlarges the committee with persons not designated by the church.

4. Don't make assumptions that the church will automatically accept the committee's recommendation.

5. Don't allow a candidate to make a decision and take actions to resign or move until after the church has voted.

6. Don't publicize decisions to call or votes to call a staff person prematurely.

7. Don't assume anything. Check out all information given by the prospective staff person.

8. Don't use the new position just to help out a friend (preacher or otherwise) who needs a job.

A pastor and personnel committee who do their homework in studying the needs for an additional staff member, who respond to the expectations of the church, who count the costs, and who discover and build congregational support will be able to interview potential candidates with the assurance that they are representing the church faithfully. A pastor, personnel committee, and candidate for the staff position who work together in openness and prayer will build the foundation for an effective and rewarding shared ministry.

---

[1]Jerry Brown, _Church Staff Teams That Win_ (Nashville: Convention, 1979), p. 56.

Appendix

STAFF DEVELOPMENT STUDY

_____ Baptist Church

Church Survey

Our church is conducting a survey to determine the need for an additional staff member. Conditions seem to indicate the need for a full-time position. We are presently studying the growth trend in membership and attendance for Sunday School and the church. We are looking at our budget. An important part of our consideration is your expectations. We are asking you to complete this survey form so that we can know your thinking. Turn the survey in at the close of our meeting today.

1. What do you expect a new staff member to do?

_____

_____

2. What will be the most important duty?

_____

_____

What will be the second most important duty?

_____

_____

What will be the third most important duty?

_____

_____

3. What is your thinking concerning the role of the pastor and a new staff member?

_____

_____

JOB DESCRIPTION
(Illustration Only)

Minister of Education

Principal Function

The minister of education is responsible to the pastor for the development and promotion of Sunday School, Church Training, missions, and administrative services of _____ _____ Baptist Church.

Responsibilities

1. Lead in planning, organizing, staffing, conducting, and evaluating a comprehensive program of religious education.

2. Lead in enlisting volunteer leaders for church programs and church committees in cooperation with the nominating committee.

3. Lead in developing training plans and programs for volunteer leaders in cooperation with the Church Training program.

4. Supervise work of assigned paid staff members.

5. Supervise maintenance of personnel records of paid staff members; implement church adopted personnel policies and procedures.

6. Edit and produce church newsletter, bulletin, and promotional material.

7. Prepare ministry action budgets with assigned programs; coordinate budget preparation with stewardship committee; manage approved budget for assigned areas

8. Serve as purchasing agent for the church as assigned.

9. Serve on the Church Council.

10. Organize and develop a churchwide visitation program.

11. Perform other duties as assigned by the pastor.

(This illustration presents some ideas for a job description. The job description for your position needs to describe the relationships and work needed in your church.)

JOB DESCRIPTION
(Illustration Only)

Minister of Education and Music

Principal Function

The minister of education and music is responsible to the pastor for the development of Sunday School, Church Training, missions programs, Music Ministry, and the administrative services program of the church.

Responsibilities

1. Direct the planning, coordinating, promoting, operating, and evaluating of educational, music, and administrative programs.

2. Lead in developing volunteer leaders in cooperation with the church nominating committee.

3. Supervise the work of assigned paid staff members.

4. Assist chairpersons of church committees.

5. Prepare annual ministry action budgets for assigned programs for approval; administer approved budget.

6. Assist the pastor in planning worship services and special events.

7. Produce and edit church newsletter and promotional brochures.

8. Organize and direct a churchwide visitation program.

9. Serve on the Church Council.

10. Lead in developing training plans for elected church leaders.

11. Serve as purchasing agent for the church as assigned.

12. Work with association and state leaders in planning and promoting leader training and program development.

(This illustration presents some ideas for a job description. The job description for your position needs to describe the relationships and work needed in your church.)

88573